IAN T. WERRETT

How We Are Failing the Right to Education

and how we can fix it

Contents

To all of my teachers.
(From school, university and in my career.)

A Note From The Author

I have spent my career trying to help at-risk young people. I have worked with asylum seeking children, refugee children, stateless children, differently abled children, kids caught up with crime, kids who have survived trauma and those from the lower socio-economic strata of our global society. I have been lucky enough to attend four universities and deepen my understanding of politics, human rights law and education.

All of the children I have worked with, despite their varying obstacles in life, shared a desire to go to school and learn. Thank you for picking up this book and showing your support for everybody's right to education.

Some of my personal experiences will pop up in this book when relevant. Each chapter will also contain one, or more, flashbacks from my time as an aid worker sharing first hand tales of those far less fortunate than ourselves.

I hope you'll enjoy this book and learn something new.

Thank you so much.

Ian T. Werrett

@iantwerrett

List of Abbreviations

- ACHR – American Convention on Human Rights
- AfCHPR – African Charter for Human and Peoples' Rights
- APR – appeal rights exhausted
- ASEAN – Association of South-East Asian Nations
- C of E – Church of England
- CRC – Convention on the Rights of the Child
- EAC – Educate a Child
- ECHR – European Convention on Human Rights
- ECtHR – European Court of Human Rights
- ESOL – English for Speakers of Other Languages
- FE – further education
- FSM – free school meals
- GCSE – General Certificate of Secondary Education
- GNP – gross national product
- ICC – International Criminal Court
- ICCPR – International Covenant for Civil and Political Rights
- ICESCR – International Covenant for Economic, Social and Cultural Rights
- ILO – International Labour Organisation
- IMF – International Monetary Fund
- NGO – non-governmental organisation
- ODA – official development assistance

- OECD - Organisation for Economic Co-operation and Development
- UCU - University and College Union
- UDHR - Universal Declaration of Human Rights
- UN - United Nations
- UNESCO - United Nations Educational, Scientific and Cultural Organization
- UNHCR - United Nations High Commissioner for Refugees
- UNICEF - United Nations Children's Fund

1

Religion, Nazis and the United Nations

Where do human rights come from?

O n one of the first days of my postgraduate degree, we were invited to muse over the idea that human rights began with religion. The reason for this is that religion may provide the first historic documents in which certain rights were written down and issued as law. We may believe that there had been rights before this, known between people and communities. But perhaps religion is seen as the earliest example of power and authority being used to protect people. For example, one could opine that 'thou shalt not kill' has evolved to mean that any attempt to kill someone must be investigated and punished by law, as the government must protect the 'right to life'. Thus 'thou shalt not kill' was a precursor to the 'right to life'.

Another argument for the development of human rights could be linked to democracy. Democracy invites us to participate in government rather than be ruled over by the whims of a tyrant, both promoting freedom and equality. Thus, the ancient Greeks could have played a vital role in the promotion of human freedom and equality as they believed in popular rule and equal participation. Certain human rights, formally written down centuries later, would guarantee ideas key to democratic rule, such as the right to take part in government.

We may believe that rights exist regardless of official documentation. We can be sure that within a community people treat one another with basic respect due to their beliefs as to what is right and what is wrong. If you remove the 'right to life' or scrap 'thou shalt not kill' very few individuals would change their habits about murder. However, one key issue regarding human rights is that we, the people, are the rights holders, and governments are the duty bearers. It is the government that has an obligation to protect these rights; people need to enjoy them. Whether this all stems from religion, democracy, or both, the structure of international human rights law as we know it today kicked off at the end of World War Two.

It was following the Nazi government's abhorrent treatment of people that the victors of the war drafted the Universal Declaration of Human Rights (UDHR). This declaration, however, is just that, a declaration – meaning it is not legally binding but merely aspirational. All the nations in the United Nations (UN) have agreed to sign up to these aspirations. But creating legally binding human rights was somewhat more troublesome and has produced a multiplicity of documents over the decades. We shall briefly look at different kinds of international laws and the structure that upholds them to better guide us in understanding what we mean when we talk about human rights. A full, academic and detailed account can be found elsewhere, such as in the work of Malcolm N. Shaw.[1]

After the UDHR had been signed, nations set about trying to create the legally binding documents that would enact its aspirations. Certain states felt that civil and political rights were most important; they wanted to ensure that all people were free to challenge and question their governments, and live free from discrimination. On the other hand, other nations felt that economic, social and cultural rights were more important; they wanted to ensure that people had enough to eat and had access to adequate housing, among other rights. This resulted in the creation of two treaties: the International Covenant for Civil and Political Rights (ICCPR) and the International Covenant for Economic, Social and Cultural Rights (ICESCR). These two key documents remain the cornerstone of human rights law today. They are both examples of treaty law – the law that has been written down and to which nations have signed up. Treaty law is simply an agreement to do something between nations which has been put in writing. In terms of human rights treaties, the UN tends to draft these and keep hold of these treaties; they also keep an eye on nations' adherence to them (more on this later).

The second kind of human rights law that we enjoy, after international treaties, is protected by customary law. Customary law stemmed from a very difficult question posed after World War Two. If the UN was founded after World War Two and the treaties protecting our rights were only written and signed years later, how could anyone argue that the Nazis had breached anyone's human rights? After all, the Holocaust was legal under German law, and no international treaty law banning it existed at the time. Furthermore, the Nazis had removed the legal status of Jewish people by depriving them of citizenship, thus stripping away their legal protection concerning the rights of German citizens.[2] However, justice was delivered thanks to a different kind of international law – that of customary law. Customary law asserted that, because countless governments around the world believed that the actions of the Nazis were illegal, that made it illegal (and that it had always been illegal and not just retrospectively). This may seem a bit odd. It may seem like it goes against the idea that a nation should decide for itself what is legal and what is not. However, if many nations act similarly, and they all believe that something should be followed as a rule or law, then another nation should not break the unwritten rule – even in regard to its own people.

We should imagine this logic in a hypothetical situation with a group of people. Imagine there are 20 people in a room and 20 plates of food on the table in the middle of the room. Nineteen of these people believe that they should not take food from more than one plate, nor should they throw their food at anyone else. Then, imagine that one person thinks differently, and they start to take food from as many plates as they like, and they throw food at some of the other people. It would be natural for that person to face some consequences. There is logic if one country harms another country but it's not the same as punishing Germany for the treatment of their own people. Next, imagine a street with ten families living on it, in an imaginary place with no written laws. On this street, nine of the households believe that they should feed and care for their children; they all do this and they all believe it should be expected as a rule. One household decides to starve and beat their children. Logic states that this household should face some consequences for their actions. When rules exist like this it is known as customary law. One such customary law is the principle of non-refoulement. This means that if you apply for refugee status in a country that country cannot simply kick you out or force you back to your home nation where you may be in danger of persecution.

This is where our rights come from, in a legal sense – either treaty law or customary law. Over time, international treaties have multiplied, with treaties concerning the treatment of certain demographics, such as women, indigenous people, disabled people and migrant workers. There is a wealth of international documents – legally binding pieces of statute that exist purely to limit the power of government and protect the well-being of people.

Regional treaties (and organisations to administer them) have emerged too. Prime examples include the European Convention on Human Rights (ECHR), the African Charter for Human and Peoples' Rights (AfCHPR) and the American Convention on Human Rights (ACHR). These regional treaties all come with their own courts to oversee the implementation of the treaties and ensure that some form of power exists beyond any single government's reach. Again, these are voluntary; countries decide if they want to join or not and, if they join, they agree that the relevant court can keep an eye on them and potentially make judgements regarding their government's behaviour seeking or enforcing change. The Association of South-East Asian Nations (ASEAN) have gone as far as to make a human rights declaration, but have not yet managed to create a treaty. Although a declaration is aspirational and not legally binding it is still to be celebrated as a move in the right direction. These regional treaties are not held by the UN, but rather by the regional organisations themselves. The UN might refer to them from time to time, but they are not the ones who have the final say about whether and how nations follow a regional treaty.

When discussing these international and regional treaties

with students, some of them ask why the UK cannot have its own set of rules. Amidst the zeitgeist of Brexit, one could be forgiven for thinking that national sovereignty was of paramount importance. Indeed, national democracy and accountability are key political concepts, and the idea of a treaty and court existing outside of any one nation, with no elected official overseeing it, may sound a little 'backwards'. But these ideals, these rights, have been fought for by countless people who wanted to protect their rights. Once these rights become the norm in a society, that society feels they should be expanded to other nations. It was not too long ago that gay marriage was unlawful in the UK. Now many in the UK feel that equal marriage should be available globally. We must not forget the horrendous events that kick-started all this – Germany's treatment of its people under Nazi rule. By making the laws international, we limit the power of governments to abuse their people. We do not limit the power of governments to provide for or protect their people. We are the benefactors here, and it is incredibly difficult to find a human right that you would want your government to remove. For example, would you like to remove freedom from torture? That would mean that you hand your government the legal ability to torture people, possibly including you. How about removing the right to freedom of expression? Once it is removed, however, you may not be free to express support or opposition to its loss. If a government treats its people well, then there is no need to remove any international human rights laws, as they are all followed. If a government does not treat its people well, then it is important to have the international laws in place to protect people.

The aforementioned treaty laws and customary laws are the rights we should be concerned with, and aim to understand and protect. I do not recognise people who use the term 'human rights' to cover all forms of human treatment. Lots of people can shout about their rights – but if they do not know what they are, they may just be shouting rubbish. For example: 'I want to go into this shop now, to buy a bottle of water because it is my basic human right!' Except it is not; you do have a right to water, what exactly that means can vary depending if your country has signed the relevant treaty. The right to water means access to water from the government, not any particular shop you demand it from. So long as the government ensures you have access to water, and certainly does not prevent you from accessing water, then your rights are being upheld. Another somewhat worrying, but thankfully disappearing, trend is to create fictitious rights to support your own nonsense. Nick Griffin, a former far right political party leader in the UK, tried to assert that people have a 'right to discriminate'.[3] This certainly does not exist, not in terms of either treaty law or customary law. We all enjoy freedom *from* discrimination as a right but certainly not the antithesis that Mr Griffin had hoped for.

To sum up the discussion thus far:

- World War 2 Two kick-started a number of activities aimed at protecting our rights.
- We enjoy our rights; governments need to uphold and protect them.
- Human rights can be in the form of treaty law, i.e., written down and agreed to.
- Human rights can be in the form of customary law, i.e., enough nations practise something and act as though it is a law.

This has been an introduction to the UN. The UN will come up a lot as they play a pivotal role in international human rights law. I hope that this study's introduction to the UN was more pleasant than my own personal introduction to the UN.

At the first UN event I attended I was immediately put out of sorts by needing to use the lavatory just minutes before the conference began. I nipped into the hotel toilets, completed my desired action and tried to flush. I was used to either a hole in the ground or a Western-style toilet, with a simple pull or push flush. On this occasion, however, I was in a hotel way beyond my financial means. It had marble floors and very high ceilings. I tried in vain, pressing various buttons, to try and flush the toilet. Eventually, I saw a button that sported an image of water and thought I had cracked the porcelain enigma. I leaned over the bowl and pushed the button only to be greeted by a small plastic pipe emerging from the bowl that sprayed my face with water. The in-built bidet designed to cleanse the world's most esteemed backsides had splashed water all over my face minutes prior to my introduction to the UN. I used the air-pressured hand dryer to dry my face, squatting down and looking up at the dryer as a possible ambassador or government secretary entered the room and looked on aghast. I was at this function to represent someone working in the human rights field, I hope the impression I made went beyond the bathroom.

How do international human rights work?

When it comes to international law, a country voluntarily approves of a treaty. This is known as ratification. The treaty is then legally binding upon that country and the treaty shall be performed in good faith; this is known as *pacta sunt servanda* (the language of law includes a lot of Latin, I will try not to use too much in this book unless it is absolutely necessary).[4]

Many of these treaties have monitoring bodies, which oversee the implementation of the treaties and interpret the law. When you agree to a treaty you agree that the treaty-monitoring body are the experts who check you are following the treaty. This is part of the treaty package. Remember, these laws are there to protect us from governments, so it makes sense that someone needs to keep an eye on the governments and check they are following the rules.

What is unfortunate, however, is that if a country chooses not to adhere fully to an international treaty it can make a 'reservation', where it tells the relevant treaty body (often a sub-body of the UN) that it does not agree with certain listed requirements, numbered as articles, of the treaty. For example, Saudi Arabia has a reservation on Article 9 of the Convention on the Elimination of all Forms of Discrimination against Women. This means that Saudi Arabia will not grant women equal rights to men concerning the nationality of their children.[5] One would imagine that there are a fair few other articles in that treaty that the government of Saudi Arabia are not upholding as well. The important thing here is that there are no real consequences for this; it is perfectly legally fine to make a reservation like this. The country may suffer a little bit of international embarrassment, or need to put up with some flak

9

from other nations; but legally they are good to go. Unless they try to make a reservation on something that is regarded as a pre-emptive norm. Pre-emptive norms, or *jus cogens* to give them their Latin name, are customary laws that cannot be in any way relaxed or applied with exceptions. These include rights such as freedom from torture or slavery.

Even if a country does not make a reservation and still chooses not to adhere to the articles, the worst it might receive is a harshly worded letter from the UN. A few of these letters is fine – almost every country gets a telling off from UN treaty bodies. But if you get lots of tellings off from the UN then countries start to take notice. This is made manifest when those with the purse strings might start to block or restrict trade with your country. Make some changes and treat your people better and, hey presto, trade restrictions are lifted. Refuse to make changes, continue to abuse your own people's rights and you may end up as a point of discussion for the UN Security Council. This is when it can get really serious. The UN Security Council is a group of nations that can legally decide to use force. Do as they say and you will be alright – refuse to do as they say and they might just agree to send in their militaries. It is often not that simple though as there are five permanent members on the Security Council and they each have veto power. These five members are the US, UK, France, Russia and China. Because of diplomatic relations and geography, China will likely always veto action against North Korea – that is one reason the Kim dynasty seems to get away with a plethora of human rights abuses. The same may be argued regarding Israel's behaviour and their protection from the US. International law binds closely with politics and diplomacy.

So international law is a bit of a funny case as it is legally binding but often not enforceable. In other words, who would run an international court to decide what is legal and what is not? We have the International Court of Justice, but it cannot issue legally binding judgements. Instead, it offers 'advisory opinions'. Essentially, the court will determine whether or not a nation has broken the law but it cannot force a government to change anything and it only has specific circumstances when it can make those rulings. This is known as 'jurisdiction'. These rulings, however, may lead to international embarrassment for the state involved; or, at times, they can simply provide a decent means of arbitration between two countries. A far worse fate would be to anger the Security Council who could use military power to force change.

There is also, however, the International Criminal Court (ICC). This court does not look at the actions of countries, but at the actions of people, issuing arrest warrants for people who commit genocide, war crimes or crimes against humanity. These involve the most heinous human rights violations and look at the most senior individuals who may be responsible. So long as the perpetrator's nation or the victims' nation has signed up to the Rome Statute (the treaty that established the ICC) then they may face trial for their actions. There are other criteria to meet, such as the gravity of the offence and the interest of justice, but if the ICC is satisfied then an individual could go away for a very long time. One big advantage here is that it means a government official or powerful oligarch cannot simply plead immunity, or bribe a corrupt judge and get away with it. Sitting heads of state, however, may refuse to cooperate and try to barricade themselves into their own country to avoid trial. It looked like the ICC was due to prosecute a head of state when Uhuru Kenyatta was initially summoned facing charges of crimes against humanity in 2011. Before the case could reach a conclusion, Mr Kenyatta assumed the office of presidency of Kenya in 2013. Roughly one month prior to his inauguration, however, the ICC withdrew charges against him due to lack of evidence.[6]

Summing up this part of the chapter:

- Governments can make a reservation about certain rights when they sign up to a treaty.
- Human rights treaties have monitoring bodies that oversee the adherence to a treaty.
- Monitoring bodies and the international court of justice can recommend changes to state practice, but not legally enforce them.
- Enforcement may come about through a mix of diplomatic, political and financial decisions and actions taken by the UN or individual nations.
- The ICC deals with people, not countries, and can arrest people.

The impossible balancing act

Enforcing change when a government violates people's rights is a bit of a mixed bag. Mostly, though, it all starts with the monitoring bodies that oversee the adherence to a treaty. We should take a look at an example of one of those monitoring bodies giving a nation a telling off. In 1969 the UK ratified the International Convention on the Elimination of All Forms of Racial Discrimination. The treaty's monitoring body, the Committee on the Elimination of Racial Discrimination, found the following, regarding the UK media in October 2016:

- ''In particular, the Committee is deeply concerned that the [Brexit] referendum campaign was marked by divisive, anti-immigrant and xenophobic rhetoric, and that many politicians and prominent political figures not only failed to condemn such rhetoric but also created and entrenched prejudices, thereby emboldening individuals to carry out acts of intimidation and hate towards ethnic or ethno-religious minority communities and people who are visibly different.
- The Committee also remains concerned at the negative portrayal of ethnic or ethno-religious minority communities, immigrants, asylum seekers and refugees by the media in the State party, particularly in the aftermath of terrorist attacks...''[7]

Oh dear. When it comes to upholding this treaty, it looks like the UK has been asked to sit on the naughty step. However, if we had tried to limit the actions of the media then that might be a problem regarding freedom of expression. This is an example of when certain rights can conflict – a difficult balancing act needs to be made in each and every society. In the UK, should we put restrictions in place on the media regarding their headlines and stories concerning minorities? If so, where exactly do we draw that line? Should we ban newspapers from naming ethic groups? Should we ban them from naming anyone's ethnicity and instead focus only on the story? Should they be banned from reporting negatively on how migration affects the public purse?

13

What if the same story has positive facts – then do we allow it?

Another example of this balancing act came when someone called Mr Lee wanted a cake. However, Mr Lee wanted a cake, from a Christian bakery, decorated with the words 'support gay marriage'. You can see the issue. The bakery refused to make Mr Lee the cake. Mr Lee has been discriminated against, you may cry. But wait – the Christian bakery should be free to practise their values and beliefs, you may equally scream. This particular case ding-donged back and forth until it found its way to the UK Supreme Court. They ruled that freedom of expression also includes the freedom to not be forced to express anything you do not want to – and the bakery wished not to express this opinion. It also found that the bakery chose not to make the cake due to the message, not because of Mr Lee's sexuality; thus he, as an individual, had not been discriminated against.[8] Mr Lee has decided to take his case to the European Court of Human Rights (ECtHR) … making this one very expensive cake. After people have exhausted their options for justice in their own country, they can take their case to the ECtHR, so long as their country is a member of the ECHR. By going to the ECtHR you have a check for your rights beyond the reach of your own government – a fairly strong check to make sure our rights are protected. (Note, the ECtHR is not part of the EU so Brexit should not affect this.)

What are the limits on our rights?

There are two key areas I want to look at here: those of abso-lute versus qualified rights and those of derogable and non-derogable rights (we'll explain what these mean shortly). We enjoy all of them, but their strength varies.

Firstly, we should look at absolute rights versus qualified rights. An absolute right is a right that is applied with no exceptions. A good example here is the right to life. If a nation does not have the death penalty, then the right to life in that nation is an absolute right. In such a nation there is no legal route to remove someone's life. If you are sick you must be treated, if you are murdered it must be investigated and, no matter what crime you commit, the government cannot take your life.

In a nation that does have the death penalty, however, the right to life is a qualified right. Essentially this is saying that 'you have the right to life unless...' In such a country the government has an obligation to protect your right to life unless you are found guilty of having committed certain crimes.

The death penalty is a topic that always brings up interesting debates in a classroom. Some view it as draconian, and rightly assigned to a less enlightened past. However, one of the beautiful things about being a teacher is that I am always allowed to play devil's advocate – so on the rare occasion when no student dissents from the aforementioned norm I can ask some very unpleasant questions. For example, if someone planned to kill your family, and carried out the act, whilst fully conscience of their actions, would you be comfortable knowing that your tax money was feeding and sheltering that individual in prison for decades to come? If someone commits murder, with no room for doubt in the conviction, such as the terrorist who murdered worshippers in mosques in New Zealand, is it fair that he will still breathe fresh air, see sunlight and enjoy visits from loved ones while countless families mourn? How can someone atone for murder whilst still enjoying their own life?

Sometimes, however, the class will go in the other direction. One student may make a case for the death penalty, similar to the arguments stated, and others seem to agree that, yes, in certain circumstances the state should have the power to end someone's life. Here, the tricky questions I pose may be as follows. What if that individual had an undiagnosed mental illness? What if the individual was groomed or brainwashed and could have, over time, given you vital information to locate and tackle the hierarchy of terrorist networks? What if, in just one in a thousand cases, the conviction is wrong? Would you be happy to know that, on average, one out of every thousand people sentenced to death was innocent? What about the case of the Nazis who were sentenced to death – would it be more powerful today to see these old feeble men, living for decades with the consequences of their actions?

Defining the limits of qualified rights can be difficult and, again, each society must find what it is happy with, or perhaps what it will tolerate. Freedom of expression is another prickly issue. Should I be free to shout racist abuse at someone in public? Should I be allowed to shout racist abuse at someone in my home? Should I be free to say racist things to my mate in the pub? Should I be allowed to say racist things to my family, in my home? Should I be allowed to post racist thoughts online? Should I be allowed to discuss racism with a stranger on the bus? Should I be free to discuss racism with a colleague at work? Should I be free to discuss racism in my home? Do any answers to the above questions change if I am a police officer, CEO, judge, nurse, journalist or teacher? Everyone will have their own answers to the above questions, and society also needs to draw a line somewhere.

Secondly, we should look at derogable and non-derogable

rights. Derogable rights are rights that are allowed to be somewhat relaxed in times of emergency. This means that the authority, strength or power of the right can be lessened or restricted, in proportionate response to the emergency, or as the ICCPR puts it 'strictly required by the exigencies of the situation'.[9] Rights contained in the ECHR, the ICCPR and the ACHR all allow for certain rights to be derogated from. The rationale behind this is that governments may need to shift their focus or deal with limited resources during a time of war or public emergency threatening the life of the nation.

For example, when the UK was dealing with numerous terror attacks due to the conflict in Northern Ireland they were allowed to derogate from certain judicial rights, concerning the speed with which someone is brought before a judge and the time they should wait for a trial. Suspected terrorists had been detained for up to 7 seven days before any judicial intervention. Previously, the European Court had stated that anything longer than four days was unlawful. This seven-day detention was allowed because the UK had formally declared the emergency to the Council of Europe (they oversee the treaty and the court), and they were found to have derogated to an extent that was acceptable within the situation. As the UK was battling with terror attacks threatening the lives of countless citizens, this change to the rules was allowed.[10]

Once the emergency is over, derogations too must cease. There are certain rights, as mentioned earlier, which are recognised as international pre-emptive norms – things that pretty much everyone agrees should be protected – and these cannot be derogated from. Any right that cannot be derogated from is a non-derogable right, essentially meaning that no matter what hardship the government is facing it must uphold its obligations as duty bearers of these rights.

To sum up this section:

- Some rights are absolute, meaning they do not have any exceptions.
- Some rights are qualified, meaning that you have the right, unless...
- Defining exactly the extent of our rights may change from society to society.
- Some rights are derogable meaning they can be relaxed in proportion to an emergency.
- Some rights are non-derogable – no relaxing, no way, no how.

What are fundamental human rights?

Honestly, I have no idea. The answer seems to vary between countries and cultures. We know what treaty rights are. We know what customary rights are. We know what absolute rights are. We know what qualified rights are. We know what derogable rights are. We know what non-derogable rights are. But, from my point of view, I do not know what 'fundamental' human rights are. My main worry about this term is that it seems to imply there are human rights that are not fundamental – which ones are those? Which are the human rights that we could do without? I think this is more of a political phrase, or a phrase used to grab people's attention. With some curiosity and concern, I have taken a brief pause from writing this paragraph to reach for dictionaries on my shelf to look up the word 'fundamental'. Fundamental does not appear in my law dictionary. According to my *Oxford English Dictionary* it means 'of basic importance'. All human rights, in my opinion, are of basic importance and thus none should ever be considered as not being fundamental. I do not, though, wish to belittle or deter those who do fight for 'fundamental' human rights. The majority of them do amazing work and perhaps their literary licence, employing a potentially defunct yet emotive adjective, implores a more sympathetic ear.

Flashback: I am in a freshly painted light yellow room, sitting on a sofa, opposite a dimly lit corridor. My tired body sinks into the soft cushions as I notice a small kitchen area next to the corridor. Sat next to me is my future boss as she explains to me the challenges facing the children she works with. We are in her children's centre, with the air-conditioning turned on to keep us cool from the humid Southeast Asian air. I can hear the children playing and laughing upstairs. As she explains that some of the children had been bought and sold, I feel a sense of pain in my stomach at the pure injustice contained in her words. My heart drops as she informs me that some of the children had been used as sex slaves and raped multiple times a day. The cruelty of her tales are in contrast with the kindness in her voice, as it becomes clear this is what had driven her. One little girl, aged about six or seven, walks past us, drinking water from a plastic cup. Our conversation pauses as we look at the child, smile and wave at her. Despite believing she cannot understand English it seemed only natural to place such a discussion on hold around such delicate and innocent ears. Hearing these stories and seeing the children up close forces me, for the first time during my career, to go into 'robot mode'. In 'robot mode' I can take in all the information I need and place my emotions to one side, coming back to them later. After getting the facts about what is happening to trafficked children, we head upstairs so that I can introduce myself to the kids. We ascend the staircase, turn a corner and are greeted by numerous little ones laughing, playing and cursorily looking up to see the new adult in the room. I look out at a room full of smiling and happy children, in painful and stark contrast to the information I have just received.

With this understanding of human rights, and what we are talking about here, next we should look at the right to education. What exactly does that particular right mean?

2

The World, Europe, Africa, The Americas and Asia

How important is this right?

As an educator, I could assert my own beliefs regarding the right to education as the cornerstone of a society that allows for an individual to strive towards independence and fulfil their potential. Having worked with young people denied this right, it was one of the key things I wished I could have provided for them. To see all children in school, to know that no child was denied the right would set a firm and increasingly fair bedrock from which societies could grow.

Education also emerges as a core need amongst those fleeing or surviving conflict. After people were liberated from Nazi concentration camps, many were housed as displaced people in camps created by the allied powers. The displaced persons began to create makeshift schools and adults of the community provided lessons.[11] After surviving the horrors of genocide people still felt that education was a vital resource and took it upon themselves to provide this. I have witnessed similar programmes set up by communities fleeing persecution from the Burmese military.

The Committee on Economic, Social and Cultural Rights, the UN monitoring body for the ICESCR, assert that education is not just an indispensable right in itself but that it is also an indispensable means of attaining other rights. The right to education empowers people who may be marginalised, socially and economically, to lift themselves out of poverty.[12] The committee goes on to provide a beautiful and poetic, yet succinct and unarguable, truth regarding the right to education:

''a well-educated, enlightened and active mind, able to wander freely and widely, is one of the joys and rewards of human existence.''[13]

I could not have put it better myself – which is why I did not try. When we pause during our daily tasks to ponder, query and daydream, are these intimate and personal experiences not made richer by being one of the lucky ones, with an educated mind? When we economically plan for our families and our future, how often do we, unknowingly, refer back to our maths teacher's lessons? When we build new friendships and form complex relationships, how much do we owe to overcoming these same difficulties in our first years at primary school?

Perhaps one of the best ways to appreciate the significance of this right is via a brief mental exercise. Imagine planning your finances without even primary level maths skills. Imagine looking, and applying, for work void of literacy skills. Imagine trying to visit other parts of the world, without the skills to fill in a form and apply for a passport. Imagine all that you gained from school, college or university – then imagine waking up tomorrow with it all gone. How would your life change?

What does the international right to education mean?

We should start by focusing on international law, as we are looking at the right to education globally. I am unaware of any customary law regarding the right to education. However, the right has appeared in many legal documents between nations. If we remember, the UDHR is the aspirational document, setting out rights and freedoms that nations agree to aspire to when they join the UN. The UDHR asserts that everyone has the right to education – but what education exactly? According to the UDHR, elementary education shall be free and compulsory. Technical and professional education shall be made generally available and higher education shall be equally accessible to all based on merit.[14]

Looking at the aspirations set for the right to education, it seems pretty absolute for elementary education, as it is free and compulsory. However, legal researchers like very clear and definite language and, when it comes to technical and professional education, 'generally available' is not particularly reassuring. Higher education talks of access upon 'basis of merit', which seems to be the norm; universities have criteria for admission and do not have to accept people in the same way a primary school does.

It is difficult to know where, morally, one could draw a line regarding accessibility for education. Primary education being open to all is something that does not require much convincing, save for the occasional bigot or misguided zealot. What about secondary education, which seemed to be missing from the UDHR? Should that be compulsory and free for all? It is in the UK – but then we are a wealthy nation; we can afford this. Some people have argued that teenagers might value their education more if they needed to pay directly for it, rather than through tax. I am not convinced by this argument because I feel that a young person's future should not be disadvantaged by their parent's financial situation. Having said that, many seem content that tertiary education should be paid for by way of fees rather than solely by taxes. In the UK it seems entrenched that secondary education is free, yet tertiary education incurs life-long debt for the graduate. Is this perhaps too drastic a change from one level to the next? It could explain some of the snobbery around attending university, as prestige often accompanies price.

For myself, I have tried to be thankful for my university education and aware that other people, perhaps far more academically gifted than me, simply could not afford this educational opportunity. It was during my undergraduate degree that I studied numerous government systems around the globe, researched international relations and learned how to neck a bottle of red wine whilst playing drunken football in a Japanese park! It was during my postgraduate degree that I studied international human rights law and learned that simply being a student cannot reverse the ageing process, as I nodded off in a night club surrounded by far younger peers. Being suddenly awoken by an inebriated stranger in their early 20s shouting in your face is not a graceful way to acknowledge your limitations. I am, too, as are many, guilty of not making the most of all the educational advantages that were laid before me. Part of the university experience, however, is learning who you are as an adult, exploring your limitations free from parental oversight.

In terms of compulsory education, the question is, when should it end? Can someone say that they have all the necessary educationally attained tools to survive independence upon completion of primary school? I would argue not. I worked in a primary school for just under two years and would say that, upon graduation, if we can call it that, pupils were certainly less likely to misuse capital letters, get confused by basic mathematical problems or glue their ear to their shoulder – but they were perhaps not ready to manage a household budget. Secondary education can provide someone with the analytical, mathematical and literary skills to survive and even thrive. Some people who have struggled at school flourish in the workplace. This is something I begrudgingly accept as a teacher – that education beyond essential skills is not always the best route for everyone. Thus, I accept the argument that technical, professional and higher education should be open to all, but not compulsory.

After the UDHR, numerous legally binding treaties guaranteeing the right to education have been discussed, written and agreed upon. They should provide some more clarity as to what exactly this right guarantees. The right to education is included under both the ICCPR and ICESCR. The ICCPR asserts that parents and legal guardians have the right to make sure that their children's religious and moral education is in line with their own beliefs.[15] This seems strange to me; having worked in a Church of England (C of E) primary school I am not convinced that non-Christian parents necessarily had an alternative – they just happened to live in the catchment area. However, we can get some more detail by looking at something called a 'general comment'. A general comment is a document produced by a monitoring body to provide more explanation or clarification of certain rights contained in treaties. The monitoring body for the ICCPR has produced a general comment that helps us here. They clarify this by asserting that if a school teaches a particular faith, it must make exemptions or alternatives to accommodate the wishes of parents.[16] This means that kids can attend a faith school, different from the faith of their parents, so long as the school does not force the kids to join in religious activities or teachings. This seems more in line with what I experienced when working for a C of E school. The ICCPR is one of the treaties that allow for derogations; however, it allows no derogating from this particular right.

The ICESCR sets out some clearer guidelines for us, asserting (for clarity's sake, I have paraphrased it below) that:

- Primary education be free and compulsory for all.
- Secondary education, including technical and vocational, be made generally available and accessible to all, progressively moving towards being free. (A bit clearer but still we have that pesky 'generally available' term.)
- Higher education be accessible to all based on capacity, again progressively moving towards being free. (The UK appears to have moved backwards on this one.)
- Fundamental education be encouraged for those who had not previously completed their primary education.
- When applicable, parents and legal guardians can choose their kids' school. (Again, linking back to the parents' or guardians' beliefs.)
- If a country signs up to the ICESCR and does not yet have

compulsory and free primary education for all children, they need to submit a workable plan within two years, which they are required to adhere to, to make this happen.[17]

All this gives us some more clarity on exactly what the right to education is, and it seems somewhat of a qualified right due to the 'capacity' regarding higher education, and 'generally available' regarding secondary education. However, primary education appears as an absolute right, free and compulsory for all kids. There is also one more section of the ICESCR that I find rather interesting; I guess it also shows us something about the historical context of this document:

''The States Parties to the present Covenant recognize the right of everyone to education. They agree that education shall be directed to the full development of the human personality and the sense of its dignity, and shall strengthen the respect for human rights and fundamental freedoms. They further agree that education shall enable all persons to participate effectively in a free society, promote understanding, tolerance and friendship among all nations and all racial, ethnic or religious groups, and further the activities of the United Nations for the maintenance of peace.''[18]

For those who champion the UN, international cooperation and equality, it seems almost too perfect. Concerning the right to education, however, it is also lacking in any specific subjects or levels of attainment, – there is not much for a teacher to plan around the above grandiose quote. The monitoring body has provided more clarity on the right. Some assurance is given concerning that nebulous term 'generally available'; the

27

committee asserts that this means that secondary education is not dependent upon a student's capacity or ability and that secondary education be distributed around the country in a way that it is available to all. Furthermore, they state that making primary education free is a priority, but that once it is achieved then countries have an obligation to take concrete steps towards making secondary and higher education free also.[19]

The Convention on the Rights of the Child (CRC) also has an article dedicated to the right to education. The CRC places upon countries obligations very similar to the ICESCR, with the following differences:

- It encourages different forms of secondary education, including general and vocational.
- It takes measures to offer financial assistance in case of need, regarding the cost of secondary education.
- It makes educational and vocational information and guidance available and accessible to all children.
- It takes measures to encourage regular attendance and the reduction of drop-out rates.
- It requires that school discipline is administered in a way consistent with the child's human dignity.

Article 29 of the CRC also offers us some more information on what education is required. When we say that children have the right to free and compulsory primary education, what is to be included? According to the CRC:

"education of the child shall be directed to:

- The development of the child's personality, talents and

mental and physical abilities to their fullest potential;
- The development of respect for human rights and fundamental freedoms, and for the principles enshrined in the Charter of the United Nations;
- The development of respect for the child's parents, his or her own cultural identity, language and values, for the national values of the country in which the child is living, the country from which he or she may originate, and for civilizations different from his or her own;
- The preparation of the child for responsible life in a free society, in the spirit of understanding, peace, tolerance, equality of sexes, and friendship among all peoples, ethnic, national and religious groups and persons of indigenous origin;
- The development of respect for the natural environment."[20]

Similar to the ICESCR, it makes for poetic, and perhaps even utopian, reading. But where are the skills and competencies required for a child to attain or strive towards? The Committee on the Rights of the Child, the monitoring body that oversees the CRC, is yet to issue a general comment about the right to education. However, the United Nations Educational, Scientific and Cultural Organization (UNESCO) produced a 'World Declaration on Education for All', which was signed in Thailand in 1990. This declaration, albeit aspirational rather than legally binding, provides some more guidance in terms of what an education should include. The declaration states that:

- Primary education means that the basic learning needs of all children are satisfied.
- Countries need to define acceptable levels of learning for

educational programmes and improve and apply systems of assessment.

· Literacy programmes are vital as they are needed for accessing material for other subjects.[21]

This is the first time we see something for teachers to grab onto, essentially literacy skills need to be included, levels and assessments need to be set and primary education should meet children's basic learning needs. How one defines basic learning needs, I guess, is defined by those levels and assessments set in each country. More clarity would be nice, but there comes a point when the law needs to step back and let policy take over, especially with international law as so many countries will have different opinions. We have a clearer picture now of what this right includes. I shall come back to this later in the chapter, in the hope of being able to sum it all up in a paragraph.

Who can access the right?

It is worth noting here that numerous other international treaties mention the right to education. Notably, the Convention on the Elimination of All Forms of Discrimination against Women states that countries need to take measures to ensure that women face no discrimination and ensure women equal rights to men regarding education.[22] The Convention on the Rights of Persons with Disabilities provides numerous rights about education; I will summarise the most pertinent, aiming not to repeat what we have already covered. This convention tells us that countries need to ensure adults and children with disabilities are not excluded from education on the basis of their disability. It also states that reasonable accommodations be made, and support be in place, in an inclusive equal learning environment.[23] Other treaties, including the International Convention on the Elimination of All Forms of Racial Discrimination, the International Convention on the Protection of the Rights of All Migrant Workers and Members of their Families, and the Convention Relating to the Status of Refugees, all provide further guarantees on the right to education.[24] These treaties reinforce the obligation for countries to combat prejudice and discrimination, allowing for equal access to the right to primary education. Regarding education other than primary, no discrimination is permitted; however, the Convention Relating to the Status of Refugees asserts that refugees be treated no worse than any other non-citizen.[25] This inherently implies that there may be a difference between the treatment of citizens and non-citizens once primary education is completed. We need to address this concern.

There is a UNESCO convention entitled the Convention against Discrimination in Education. This asserts no allowance of discrimination on the grounds of race, colour, sex, language, religion, political or other opinion, national or social origin, economic condition or birth.[26] However, this makes no mention of immigration status. The International Convention on the Protection of the Rights of All Migrant Workers and Members of their Families asserts that migrant workers shall enjoy equal treatment with nationals concerning access to educational institutions.[27] Notably, this applies to migrant workers, not other migrants. Perhaps the strongest protection from discrimination when it comes to the right to education is offered by the Committee on the Rights of the Child, which asserts that the rights in the CRC, including the right to education, be enjoyed by all children 'including asylum-seeking, refugee and migrant children – irrespective of their nationality, immigration status or statelessness'.[28] This complete coverage applies to children, defined by the CRC as someone under 18 years of age unless legal adulthood is attained earlier in a given country.[29] Similarly, however, the Economic and Social Council have asserted that ICESCR rights 'apply to everyone including non-nationals, such as refugees, asylum-seekers, stateless persons, migrant workers and victims of international trafficking, regardless of legal status or documentation'.[30]

Can we wrap up this international right in a paragraph?

Elementary education, meaning basic learning needs being met, is to be free and compulsory for all people aged under 18, unless adulthood is attained earlier in that country. A country should meet this, or at least have a concrete plan on how to achieve it within two years of agreeing to it. No child should be denied this right. No child should be denied a chance to attend secondary education, including vocational and technical education; this should be generally available to all, and countries should work towards making this free. All adults should have equal access to higher education based upon merit and capacity. Once primary and secondary education are free, then countries should work towards making higher education free also. Fundamental education should be encouraged for those who did not complete their elementary education before.

Educational and vocational information and guidance should be available to all children, and discipline in schools should never violate a child's dignity. Measures should be introduced to accommodate disabled students. Measures should be taken to provide financial assistance for secondary education and encourage good attendance. I think that sums it up.

Flashback: I walk barefoot into a small one-bedroom flat that has been converted, sans budget, into a nursery for small children. The stale paint and dust fill my lungs as my heart tries not to palpitate audibly upon seeing the children's conditions. The little ones laugh and giggle as I and the other adults try to stop them from entering the kitchen, where exposed wires and building materials hang loose. All the children are asylum-seekers and I am visiting their nursery to see if there is any way my organisation can help them. The space is cramped and dangerous, but the kids are well looked after. The adults who 'work' here are paid in kind; they can sleep in the nursery in exchange for looking after the children. The staff too are asylum-seekers and it is illegal for them to work. As we gather the children for rice and water, tears are building behind my eyes. Yet I dare not let them feel daylight until I am no longer visible to minds far more innocent than my own.

Regional differences?

If a regional treaty differs from an international one, this does not mean that it can replace the international one; it acts to provide more detail, and perhaps needs, specific to that part of the world. In essence, if a country signs up to an international and a regional treaty with the same rights, they need to satisfy both. For example, if a regional treaty were to say that primary education does not need to be free, then there would still be the international law stating that it does need to be free, so it will remain free. If, however, the regional treaty says that all secondary education must be free, then even though the international law states that it does not need to be free, it would need to be free to satisfy both treaties. Looking at regional treaties can, perhaps, also show how seriously a right is taken in that part of the world, or how likely governments believe they are to meet that right.

In Southeast Asia, ASEAN does not have a legally binding treaty regarding human rights; but it has produced a human rights declaration, showing the agreed aspirations of its members. This declaration reaffirms some of the internationally agreed commitments, covering primary, secondary and higher education. The declaration refers to the rights of migrant workers but not to migrants in general. Despite a comprehensive list of protected characteristics from discrimination, there is also no explicit protection for stateless people.[31]

In Africa, the AfCHPR simply states: 'Every individual shall have the right to education.'[32] No specifics are mentioned regarding the type or level of education. The charter does provide protection from discrimination with regard to sex, race, colour, ethnicity, religion, language and political opinion, but not regarding immigration status or statelessness.[33] Although there is little detail about the right to education here, it is enshrined in a legally binding document showing some real commitment, albeit lacking in the specifics. The danger of a human right with little detail is that a government may interpret it however they like. The right to education, with no real definition, may just mean that everyone between the ages of six and nine can attend sparsely located schools for a price, or sign up and pay for online courses. In this instance, I am sure that is not the intention, but this is an example of how easy it can be to meet a human right when there is no definition of what the right means.

The definition has been provided, however, by the African Commission on Human and Peoples' Rights. The Commission urges nations to provide the opportunity for all children to enjoy free and compulsory primary education by progressively providing the finances and resources needed to achieve this end. The right to education includes pre-school, primary, secondary, tertiary, adult education and vocational training, with equal access for all persons without discrimination. The Commission calls for educational programmes that serve the needs of society and, in particular, girls, vulnerable children such as children with disabilities, refugee children, migrant children, street children, internally displaced children, pregnant children and children from marginalised communities, and to end discrimination against children with HIV/AIDS.[34] The specific communities highlighted calls for highly inclusive education that does not shy away from challenging social stigma and mentioning those children who are at high risk, perhaps reflecting the needs of communities on that continent.

In the Americas, the ACHR asks nations to work progressively towards achieving the right to education as enshrined in the Charter of the Organisation of American States.[35] The charter provides a fairly comprehensive set of guarantees for the right to education. Notably different from what is already required under international law, the charter calls for the rapid eradication of illiteracy and an expansion of educational opportunities for all, stating that the encouragement of education be of primary importance in development plans.[36] Specifics on the right itself are in line with international law, except that it asks nations to diversify secondary education in a way that meets the development needs of the country.[37] Reflecting on the overall goal of development and linking it with education highlights the importance of education in creating a skilled and capable workforce that can contribute to a nation's wealth.

In Europe, the ECHR, representing the richest grouping of nations to create a regional human rights treaty, sadly shows little commitment to the right. The right to education was added in 1952, with the first protocol to the ECHR stating that no one be denied the right to education, and also that parents can ensure their child's education be in line with their religious and philosophical convictions.[38] Why a group of wealthy nations, with all the infrastructure in place, and having already signed up to numerous international treaties could not be more specific and reaffirm their commitment to education is a bit of a mystery and somewhat disappointing. The ECtHR, however, has bolstered and clarified the right over the years, with rulings to provide a better definition and more protection. They have also produced a guide on the right that includes the protection of children from ill-treatment in schools and that someone's successful studies be recognised with a form of certification, among other guarantees. The guide asserts that the right be interpreted in harmony with international law and existing international treaties.[39] This essentially means that the right to education under the ECHR includes all the protections included under a plethora of international treaties that also contain the right. The guide also contains answers to more specific questions, based upon past cases. For example, if a student passes an entrance exam, the institution cannot annul the results after seeing the student's previous academic performances.[40] The court has ensured that the right to education be comprehensive and protected.

The regional differences are pretty stark, and there are, of course, many nations that have not joined any regional organisation that promotes human rights. This does not, in itself, mean that such nations are less committed. For example, Japan has not joined a regional human rights organisation, but it does play an active role in the UN and is a relatively free and open society. ASEAN has managed a declaration, which is fairly impressive considering that Burma is a member. Burma is currently under investigation because of its treatment of the Rohingya people. After working with Burmese refugees, I can say that the Burmese government should also be facing condemnation for its treatment of the Karen, Shan, Mon and numerous other ethnic groups. When you have a human rights pariah in your group, managing a declaration is a good start. If ASEAN can make a legally binding treaty regarding human rights this would be a real test of the will of the bloc to challenge some of its member countries. Southeast Asia is a beautiful part of the world, but also one with very diverse governmental systems and cultures; a legally binding human rights treaty may be some years, if not decades, away.

The approach in Africa has seemed a little bit of a let-down, as education could be a key way to lift the economies of Africa and help develop the continent, as noted in the American approach. However, we should praise the African approach of specifically mentioning children who might otherwise be marginalised. Europe is disappointing in this respect at first glance. The ECHR, is a legally binding human rights treaty that is applied to some of the wealthiest nations on earth, nations where government budgets are adequate to provide excellent educational opportunities. The treaty provides very little in the way of specifics; however, the ECtHR has provided ample definition and guarantees after numerous rulings and interpretations made by the court.

The American nations have displayed regional differences clearest by tailoring the right to education to meet the challenges of the region. Linking the right to development and focusing on the eradication of illiteracy are excellent concrete steps to ending generational poverty and highlighting how education not only benefits the individual but lifts the surrounding society and nation. Clear political will is shown in the document. Whether this is reflected in practice will be another thing.

Not an absolute right

The right to education is not an absolute right. I cannot argue that my right to education has been denied because I cannot afford to do a PhD. I can also not argue that my right to education was denied because I was not allowed to study politics until I went to university. However, the kids I worked with who were not allowed to attend a government-funded primary school certainly were denied the right to education. With a clearer picture of what this right is, who exactly has been denied the right? And what is the impact of it being denied?

3

262 Million Children, Life-Expectancy and Crime

How many people are denied the right?

According to the United Nations Children's Fund (UNICEF) one in five school-aged children are not accessing education. UNICEF assert that 175 million pre-primary school-age children and 262 million primary and secondary aged children are not accessing education.[41] I have learned that the UN will use verified, conservative numbers, and even have been advised in the past to double or even triple UN estimates on issues such as statelessness, refugees and people living in poverty. I am not sure to what extent I take this advice to heart, as I know from my brief encounters with the UN that they are thorough and well versed in their areas of expertise. However, one of the reasons the numbers are likely to be higher is due to the nature of the problem. When we are looking at children who are not in school, in some cases there will be little existing government documentation on these children. If the children are not in school, then there will be no school registers or academic records to go by to confirm their existence. If the children are not in school because they are stateless or an asylum-seeker then there may be no government documents to show that these people exist. How do you count the children who are not on the school register or the government's census? How can you count what is not there?

To gather such information, the UN may be relying on their own organisations. For example, the United Nations High Commissioner for Refugees (UNHCR) may have an office in Thailand where they can register all the asylum-seekers coming across the border from Burma. Then, they can ascertain how many of these children, if any, can access government-funded education. If they register, for example, 5,000 asylum-seeking children and know that none of them can access education then you have one part of the puzzle for Thailand. But what about other border crossing points? What about those who did cross at this border but did not register with the UN? What about the stateless kids born in the country? What about children held in forced labour who have deliberately not been registered? Now, imagine trying to calculate that for every country all over the world. As difficult as the puzzle may be, the UN, non-governmental organisations (NGOs) and governments around the world do some fantastic work in trying to find all these kids and provide some support for them. Keeping count of all of them is inherently difficult; but if anyone can come up with a realistic figure, I would trust the UN to do so.

Finding information on adults denied the right to education is much harder. As the right to education is not an absolute right when we look at adults there is a lot more room for governmental differences. For example, some European and South American countries provide higher education or certain higher education programmes for free. However, in many other countries, higher education comes with tuition fees that may economically exclude certain people. Higher education can also decide admissions based upon merit; thus, numerous applicants may not meet the required standard. None of these would be a denial of the individual's right to education. From what we covered in the previous chapter when it comes to adults, it would only be a denial of the right if people were turned away from higher education due to their ethnicity, gender, religious affiliation, immigration status or for some other protected characteristic we looked at. The same would apply to adults wanting to access technical or vocational courses where fees could be incurred and entry requirements in place. Thus, when looking for adults denied the right, we would need evidence of adults being denied access specifically due to a listed protected characteristic.

For example, in Iran in 2012 it was reported that 36 universities would only accept male applicants for 77-degree majors.[42] This would certainly be a denial of the right, as the government has not ensured equal access between the sexes. But does that mean that all women in Iran are denied the right to education or just those who applied for these specific courses? It is tough to say. Once a right becomes more nuanced, it is inherently difficult to quantify. It certainly means women in Iran do not have equal access, however.

Another example can be found when we look at educational attainment for people living with disabilities. A survey has found that people with disabilities are roughly half as likely to complete university. Adult literacy, measured in 36 countries in 2010, for people without disabilities, showed that just over three-quarters of the population were literate, compared with just over half for those with disabilities. One could opine that this may be due to types of disability affecting cognition or literacy levels. However, these statistics vary greatly between countries.[43] This shows us that in some cases governments have guaranteed equal access to education for disabled students, while others have not. Or at least that some nations fare better than others in this regard. The disparity in results is seen both when disabled people are children and when they are adults.

So, in terms of the number of people denied the right to education, all we can say for sure is that it is higher than UNICEF's assertion. This is because the UN would have verified their statistics, possibly leaving out communities who are untraceable or undocumented and hard to contact. Furthermore, UNICEF's number concerns children only, not adults. Although getting an accurate number regarding adults denied the right is far from an exact science, we know (given the example in Iran and the treatment of disabled people in certain countries) that it is higher than zero. UNICEF stated that 175 million pre-primary school-age children did not have access to education. However, when we looked at the right in detail there was no guarantee for pre-primary education. No access to primary and secondary is a violation, however, so UNICEF's number of 262 million children denied this access is our starting point. An exact number cannot be given, but we can be sure it is higher than 262 million.

Who is denied the right?

Regarding the nature of this quandary, we have already looked at the situation for adults. But who are the more than 260 million children denied the right? The UNICEF report that helped us reach our number asserts that one major obstacle to education is funding. Anything provided by the government, free of charge, has to be paid for somehow – it could be through taxes, loans or aid. If you have a smaller economy, there is less money to go towards public services, such as education. Compounding this problem is the fact that lower-income countries tend to have younger populations, meaning that more children need a school place and fewer work-age adults are contributing to the public purse.

Even schools in wealthy nations often complain of funding shortages. If you are lucky enough to live in a wealthier nation, imagine your local school needing to accommodate another hundred children and having to do so with half the budget. This is more of a thought experiment than an exact calculation – but it can help us see why a younger population causes issues. You have more kids needing a seat in the classroom and fewer working-age adults to pay for it. There are also challenges to an ageing population when many folks are past their working age and enjoying a well-deserved retirement. Migration can help to plug labour shortages in such situations, providing the needed tax money for public services. Nations with ageing populations, like the UK, Italy and Japan often need to attract foreign workers to balance the books. Lower-income countries can have a tougher time attracting workers from elsewhere and, if they do migrate, they could bring more children with them.

With lower income, poverty rates will also increase, which

can have a knock-on effect for school attendance. For example, imagine you live five miles from the nearest school and cannot afford a car or even a bike: will you walk your child to school each day or will you dedicate more time to work in the hope that you will be able to feed your child? For those living in the most extreme poverty, daily decisions can appear as intractable riddles that many of us would either never confront or only ponder for philosophical amusement. If you do not know where your child's dinner is coming from, would you have the motivation to get them to school – especially if you live in a rural area far from a school, and you know that farming knowledge will be more vital for their immediate survival than literacy skills?

We also need to consider the children affected by conflict. During a time of civil war or ethnic cleansing attending school may not be as accessible or important. According to international NGO Global Citizen, hundreds, potentially thousands, of schools have been destroyed by the Taliban in Afghanistan, Rohingya refugee children living in Bangladesh avoid school due to fear and only 13% of children living in the Dadaab refugee camp in Kenya have access to post-primary education.[44] I met many children in similar circumstances, who longed for education. Even before they fled their homes, living in fear of military attack, they still made the effort to go to school despite the dangers.

The children I worked with were fleeing ethnic cleansing in Burma. One of the amazing things about the right to education is that if it is there then the children will go; there is very little, if any, convincing that is needed. When the Burmese military stopped these kids from attending government schools, their local communities set up schools and the kids attended. When the military started arresting and taking away the teachers, the kids kept going, hoping that some of the teachers would remain and teach them. When the military came to ransack their homes and kidnap people, the children hid and then, when it was safe, they walked to their community school. When the military burned down their villages and they had to flee to another country, one of the first things they wanted to do was find and attend a school.

The asylum-seeking and refugee kids I worked with lived in one large communal space, often with one or two bathrooms, a kitchen, bedrooms and then one multifunctional room. That multifunctional room served as the kids' only playground because it was often too dangerous for them to play outside for fear of being found by an immigration officer. If I or another teacher showed up and started a lesson in that room, you could be sure that the toys were put away and the kids ran towards the lesson. But these kids were among many who were denied free government education because of war and conflict. Any country in a state of conflict will have little ones running for their lives and missing out on, among many things, their key educational years.

Now, I am sure that plenty of teachers and parents have read the last paragraph and thought 'not my kid/s they'll do anything to get out of a lesson'. If that is the case, what is the ultimate punishment that a school imposes? Either to be suspended or expelled from the school – the threat of which is often enough to see a change in behaviour. Even if kids are not focused on the lesson, most kids still want the social surrounding and the attention of the teacher. And even if they end the day not knowing the objectives of that lesson, they will still have had a chance to learn about social interactions, hierarchies and hopefully something related to the topics. I do believe that there is a process of 'learning to learn'. We need to know how education works and what our role as a student is before we can get the most from our studies. Outside fears can also disrupt behaviour, as a classroom could be a safe space to act out.

Another key reason people may miss out on an education is their immigration status. Some countries may ban people of a certain status from attending. This may be a ban on stateless people, it may be a ban on refugees or asylum-seekers, or it may be a ban on people who have migrated illegally and not applied for asylum. Immigration status seems to be the final acceptable means of discrimination; almost all people agree that treating someone differently because of their skin colour, religion or sexuality is unacceptable whilst simultaneously feeling that it is perfectly acceptable to treat someone differently due to their immigration status. I have never fully understood this socially acceptable form of discrimination. Many claim it is because immigrants will not contribute to the system and will take from it, i.e., they may arrive, not find work and then use the health service. But this is just a hypothetical, and a specific example; it does not reflect all, or most, immigrants by a long shot. Furthermore, if this is the reasoning, then why should a citizen be allowed to use the health service if they are unemployed or not able to work? People will also claim that immigrants have to prove themselves, or give back in order to remain in the country, whilst making no such demands on citizens. One hypothetical case I like to give students regarding this issue of citizens and immigrants is as follows.

In the UK citizenship is granted through bloodline, whilst in the Netherlands it is granted through the soil, i.e., being born in the country. Bill is born in the Netherlands and has British parents, which means that Bill can get both Dutch and British citizenship. Bob is born in Britain and has Dutch parents; this means that Bob cannot get British or Dutch citizenship. Is Bill more 'British' and more 'Dutch' than Bob and should Bill be entitled to more services and better working opportunities from both countries than Bob? This is a simplified example. In reality, Bob would have routes to citizenship, but they would not be as straightforward as Bill's and may incur fees and a mountain of paperwork. Also, Bob's chance of gaining the dual citizenship that Bill enjoyed from birth would likely remain out of reach. But I like to think this experiment makes the point that citizenship is not clear cut and should not be an easily accessible tool to determine who deserves what.

Humans are very tribal creatures and maybe we feel that we need a group to identify with in order to feel safe. Maybe one of the only socially acceptable groups left is immigration status and, as with any group, there are other 'different' groups. I also think it is no small coincidence that more often than not immigrants cannot vote and, thus, few politicians feel compelled to protect or fight for the interests of this demographic. If voters, however, can be convinced that immigrants are a threat and politicians can protect us from them then that is a no-brainer for those pursuing power. Having lived as an immigrant for some years I remember the feeling that my say or opinion was inherently less worthy or relevant to a citizen's on certain issues.

When I work in the UK, I am a contributing member of society. When I work in another country, I am stealing someone's job. Xenophobia seems to be a global issue, ironically. When I moved from Oxford to Northampton for work that was fine. But if I had moved from Poland, for example, to work in Northampton that would have somehow needed greater justification in the eyes of many. This prejudice makes it acceptable for certain kids, all over the world, to miss out on an education. Even for those who hold onto their bizarre xenophobic beliefs, knowing that the kids are missing out will surely pull at some emotional chords.

No child should be denied an education because of their immigration status. Having said that, integration is important and we can understand people's frustration with those who migrate and make no effort to adapt to their new home, especially when the migration is not forced. I remember meeting other British people living abroad who could not ask where the toilet was, or order food, in the native language. I cannot understand how someone could live in another country and not know how to ask where the toilet is! Has their ignorance of language and culture borne them invincible kidneys?

Sorry, we have lost focus. So, we should get back to the issue of those denied education. According to the Malala Fund, there are 130 million girls out of school. At first glance, this seems oddly like good news. If we know that more than 262 million kids are out of education then roughly half of them should be girls, and that would mean about 131 million. So, no bias here – girls and boys are denied education in equal numbers. Not quite. As the Malala Fund explains, there are certain reasons that girls are more severely affected; it is not just the denial of the right overall but the quality once that right is accessed that matters.

Many girls do have access to education, but their parents may deem education for a girl as a waste of time and money beyond a certain point.[45] (This was not the case for Malala Yusufzai herself, as detailed in her excellent autobiography *I am Malala*.[46]) This could be due to cultural norms or beliefs. It was not too long ago that many parents in the UK would still believe their daughter's future lie in being a wife and mother, who would be financially supported by a well-educated man. This links us to another obstacle facing girls – that of child marriage. According to ActionAid UK more than 250 million women alive today were married, often against their will, before reaching the age of 15. Their assumed role as a wife first will limit any perceived expectation of their educational desires and also limit their access as they are to support a husband, household and family.[47] Girls may have close to equal access to education, but the longevity of their academic paths, for many, is cut short through stigma and outdated beliefs.

Finally, we need to keep in mind that natural disasters can disrupt or destroy previously enjoyed educational opportunities. The 2014 earthquake in Nepal destroyed homes and schools, as did the 2004 Indian Ocean tsunami. After such disasters, education will have been inaccessible to people. This was through no fault of the government, however, and so long as a plan was created to ensure the rebuilding of schools and provision of education one could argue that the right to education was not denied. Remember when we talk about human rights – governments are the duty bearers, it is their job to uphold these rights. So, despite people losing their access to education, in the case of a natural disaster, it is not fair to say their right to education has been denied. However, in a perfect world, there could be some kind of emergency education system in place for such scenarios. We have seen how the world has adapted to learning throughout the Covid-19 pandemic, with remote learning becoming the norm and millions of children still able to access educational material. This issue has also highlighted, however, just how many kids do not have access to the necessary technology at home. This may change over time or may become a priority in the post-pandemic educational landscape. However, it does show how we can adapt and change to emergencies. Perhaps each nation could develop an emergency educational plan, to continue education in times of emergency or natural disaster, building upon the ingenuity of the response to Covid-19.

To sum up thus far. An exact number of people denied the right to education is hard to gauge, but it is definitely above 262 million. Those denied the right, are most likely:

- Those living in poverty.
- Those affected by war and conflict.
- Stateless people, or others of marginal immigration status.
- Disabled people.

Note Girls face unique obstacles that can limit their education.

Note Many may have their education disrupted or postponed due to natural disasters.

What is the impact on the child?

Lots of research on any form of child abuse centres on how it will affect a child's development and growth into an adult. However, I think we should also take some time to focus on how any such abuse or state of under-privilege affects the child, not just their potential future self. Children live very much in the present. Many children do not have the cognitive ability to hypothesise about their future, bar dream statements void of genuine concern such as 'I want to be a fire fighter'. The way that adults can see the consequences of their actions long term and worry about problems that have not yet arisen is something children are blissfully incapable of. I have seen former child sexual assault survivors run around in circles with their tongues flopping out like over-excited Labradors, struggling to contain their enjoyment at joining in a PE lesson. Those little ones were very much living in the moment. Their self-image had taken a battering, but they were not worrying about the future consequences or their traumatic past – at least, not at that moment. They were just kids running around, having fun.

One of the quickest and easiest ways to tell a child that they do not belong and that they are worth less than their peers is to stop them from going to school. When working with stateless children in Southeast Asia I could see the jealousy and anger in the children's words and actions when those of their friends who were citizens started talking about school or demonstrating their acquired literacy skills. At the time, my colleagues and I tried to provide some semblance of educational normality for the stateless children by spending a few timetabled hours with them, teaching them basic maths and literacy skills. Some schools, including the one established by my former employer set up for stateless kids, are of high quality and provide an amazing service. They have managed to attract many kids into their school and can provide a variety of activities and lessons. These schools are far from ubiquitous, sadly. Thus many stateless kids will not be enrolled. If these types of schools were the norm for stateless kids it could be a big improvement in certain parts of the world.

Children deprived of the right to education show signs of low self-worth and self-esteem, along with the obvious lack of demonstrable skills and tools acquired by their more fortunate peers. Future options may appear bleak, but the kids I worked with showed real ambition and imagination; their ability to dream seemed unhampered. I knew stateless children who wanted to be health professionals, restaurant owners and university lecturers. Their innocent inability to make the firm link between their current situation and their future was a blessing for their well-being. However, these were the lucky ones who still had excellent support systems at home and parents who promoted their child's value at every opportunity. When such home support does not exist, coupled with the denial to access education, the consequences for a child can be devastating. Some children were told from a young age that, for example, as a stateless girl, their best option to earn a living was in sex work, and to start gaining experience as soon as possible. Even making contact with these children was close to impossible. Any interaction with them seemed void of the notion that they had alternative options.

> **Flashback:** *My colleague and I are walking through the back streets of an area we know is a hot spot for sex work. The smell of sewage and piles of rubbish (a smell I later learned is also associated with rotting human flesh) go beyond merely affecting one sense and creates a horrid taste in the back of our throats. My footsteps fall beneath me as we guide our passage by moonlight. We are looking for vulnerable children amongst the thick adult night air. We stop to smoke a cigarette, merely as a prop, allowing us time to assess a situation where a young girl appears to be soliciting. She is at least 12 years our junior and surely not yet finished adolescence; we assume her to be about 14. The moonlight reflecting from her innocent eyes*

betray the harsh reality of her existence. She stands on a street corner, in a neighbourhood lined with hotels that rent rooms by the hour. An older man watches over her, standing less than one metre away at all times. We sense it has been many moons since she last smiled true joy at her own accord, yet her childish innocence still dares to creep beneath the surface of her expressionless face.

She is like a colourful daisy set to a black-and-white winter landscape.

Children denied an education also lack the safe support network a school can provide and may be targets for human traffickers and organised crime. From my experience, it is very difficult to tell if this is a direct cause or if the common factor, often that of statelessness, was the cause. Stateless children were not allowed to access education and were also at higher risk of being moved illegally from one country to another, often for the purpose of exploitation. This may have been due to the lack of safety tips kids pick up in schools and the lack of a safe place to stay with a support network outside of the family. Or it may have been due to the lack of citizenship making them more vulnerable to illegal means of transport, and families searching for opportunities. It is likely a combination of both. We shall come back to this issue later, in another chapter.

Concerning organised crime, some teenagers denied education may have little to do all day and feel somewhat peerless. With no educational background, they are also likely to struggle to find a job. If they grow up in a neighbourhood with high levels of organised crime then they will ask themselves, why not find work with them? Equally, they may be targeted by gangs who need loyal workers that are willing to work for little money.

To sum up the impact of lack of access to education on kids, they are:

- Damaged self-worth and potentially peerless.
- More susceptible to continuing family cycles of poverty and survival, such as sex work.
- More susceptible to trafficking.
- More susceptible to working within crime.

What is the impact on the adult?

An uneducated adult will find breaking the cycle of poverty far more difficult than an educated one. If they can learn a new skill or become literate then they have a chance to either branch out into a different career path from their parents or continue their studies and help their families to build up their own businesses. Some of the children I worked with, who were denied an education and grew up in poverty, learned to read and write and gained basic maths skills, among other skills, with us. We had no idea what they could do with their future – but one has become her own businesswoman and many other such children find a way to build a better life. This family's cycle of poverty may be broken by one girl's education.

Adults who are denied an education are more likely to continue in the cycle of poverty and die at a younger age. Here, however, I am cautious to associate the lack of education with lower life expectancy. Life expectancy is largely affected by the income both of the nation and the family. A poorer nation is likely to have fewer people in school, and a poorer family is less likely than a wealthier family to send children to school. Thus, it may be the financial situation affecting both educational opportunities and life expectancy, rather than education, having a direct impact on life expectancy. However, there is significant research showing that, within a wealthy nation, those with tertiary education live longer than those without due to lifestyle choices associated with higher education – e.g., lower alcohol consumption and fewer smokers.[48] Another study suggested that higher education grants improved planning skills and self-control resulting in longer life expectancy.[49]

From my experience adults who had been denied an education were more likely to get involved with crime. If you knew that almost all employers would want to know your educational background, would you not be tempted by someone offering reasonable money without needing a certificate – especially if you grew up in an area where you saw such activity daily? Those without any educational background are easy targets for gangs. They are people who may lack a secure peer group, have limited options and want a chance to impress people. Organised crime will need people on the ground doing the work that can be seen as riskier with less financial reward, and adults denied an education need a chance to learn a business skill and gain an income.

The other draw of crime is a fairly obvious one. It may not be recruitment from organised crime but rather crime as a means of survival. If you have no educational background to help you find work, you may end up one day starving with no income, and someone has left a bag of food on a bench – why not take it? Then the next week, you and your child are starving, you still have no legal income and someone's wallet is showing from their rucksack – why not take it? For many single mothers, with no educational background, they can often be left with little alternative to sex work to make sure their kids can eat. In numerous nations, this would also be considered illegal and a life of crime.

There are many issues linking poverty to larger families, but focusing on a lack of education there are two key factors I want to cover. Adults lacking an educational background are less likely to be properly educated on sexual health and family planning. Some amazing NGOs and health professionals are tackling this issue worldwide, but the knowledge gap still remains for many uneducated families. Another issue is role modelling. If you grew up in an uneducated household with lots of siblings, you are more likely to see this as a norm and prioritise having a family of your own over attaining a higher quality education, especially if you are someone denied the right to education. A lack of modelling educational values at a young age from your parents will have a knock-on effect and impact your own family planning in adulthood. It can also be a means of financial planning – if everyone has a low income then you may need more kids to pay for you in your old age. When the children are young, however, with a larger family and fewer routes into paid employment, it can become a real struggle to ensure the whole family has regular food, warmth, shelter and medical care, let alone education.

To sum up the impact of lack of access to education on adults, they are:

- More likely to continue the cycle of poverty.

- More likely to have a lower life expectancy.
- More susceptible to a life of crime.
- More likely to have large families, which they may struggle to care for.

How does it impact a community or an entire nation?

A link between lack of education and crime has been established. By denying people the right to education, governments are doing organised crime a big favour by providing them with a more easily recruited workforce. Simultaneously, the legal workforce and skilled labour market may become under-resourced. These individuals are also more likely to have larger families whom they cannot properly provide for, whilst themselves having a lower life expectancy than their educated peers. None of this provides a good outlook for the community or nation. One would assume that when people are denied education crime rates would be higher, life expectancy would be lower and the economy would needlessly suffer. It is becoming very clear why the Charter of the Organisation of American States strongly linked development to education.

Research into the impact of lack of education on communities and nations appears to bear this out. Links between lower educational attainment and higher crime rates have been demonstrated. By contrast, there are positive correlations between education and an aversion to risk, developing patience and becoming part of a more positive peer group. In other words, those who miss out on education are less likely to see the full risks involved with criminal behaviour, are less likely to develop the patience needed to work towards a goal, and are less likely to have friends around them to convince them not to carry out a criminal act.[50] Add to this what was mentioned before, about gangs targeting uneducated people and the need for an income when you cannot find legal employment, and it is easy to understand the link between education and crime.

Furthermore, the Organisation for Economic Co-operation and Development (OECD) has explained how an economy competes globally based upon the complexity of its production systems and services. The more complex, and thus more globally competitive, economies require a skilled and educated workforce.[51] Education, for a nation, is likely to result in lower crime rates and a more competitive economy. It may also encourage democratic citizenship and result in a more politically engaged population who have better tools at their disposal to make important decisions at the polling station. These citizens are also more likely to have an awareness of history and the diversity of opinions, building a more inclusive society.[52]

It is, I suppose, an issue of investment, with two key political obstacles. Obstacle number one relates to culture and public opinion surrounding minorities and access to services. If the government of country X guarantee education for all children they run little risk of upsetting voters. However, if there is an influx of asylum-seekers from country Y, then country X will need to reassure voters that these people cannot instantly enjoy all the benefits a nation can provide. Citizens, and voters, need to feel looked after and protected, and perhaps even somehow superior or special compared to non-citizens. Non-citizens, especially groups of people, can seem threatening to voters, and governments may need to limit access to state-run programmes to 'deter' these people from coming. In reality, when someone is fleeing for their life, they will flee regardless of access to healthcare or education, or other state support, in the host nation. Where people flee to, however, may be affected by the perceived support or opportunities available to them. Thus, denying immigrants, especially illegal immigrants, access to services usually appears as a form of protecting and prioritising the people who voted you into power. In the long run, however, this could cause real damage to a community.

The second political obstacle is one of cost and benefit. Investing in education and ensuring everyone has access to education would require a boost in state spending, likely through raising taxes. Raising taxes may lose you support in the short term. In addition, the long-term benefits of investing in education may not be visible come the next election – so you are out and the next guy wins after promising to cut taxes. Even in a non-democratic nation, those in power need to keep the public on their side or, at least, quell any unrest. An increase in taxes will not help, and an educated population is more likely to organise and mobilise against unjust treatment. Dictators may have an interest in limiting education.

To sum up the impact of a lack of access to education on a community or nation, they are:

- Higher levels of crime.
- Less globally competitive economy.
- Fewer democratic citizens that appreciate an inclusive society.

Millions of people are denied education and this affects children, adults, communities and nations. Governments are supposed to guarantee the right to education, but teachers are the ones in the classroom providing this right. What is it like for them in the classroom? How does the right to education view teachers and are teachers getting what is needed from governments to succeed? Legally speaking there is no right to teach. However, via the right to education, one can deduce that the right to teach is intrinsically linked, and a vital part of anyone's education. So, we should look at the right to teach next.

4

Broken Promises, Underpaid and Overworked

Why did I start teaching?

When I was working with high-risk kids in Southeast Asia, I was invited to give a ten-minute guest speech to university students. Their tutor felt that the students could benefit from hearing from a range of speakers, all working with different vulnerable communities. I had scheduled some time to write a short talk the morning before I was due at the university. But thanks to an emergency, I was left with no time to prepare. I had to scribble some key talking points on the back of a receipt as I sat in the taxi en route to the venue. I hoped that the other speakers were better prepared than me.

When I arrived at the university, I was greeted by the tutor who opened with 'Um... sorry to say that all the other speakers have cancelled. Are you okay to speak for one hour?' Either through pride, arrogance or simply compliance I nodded and then looked at the sweat-stained, scribbled notes in my hand. I entered the room, greeted by inquisitive eyes and eager minds who were freshly armed with the analytical tools of a tertiary education. I, and my crumpled receipt of bullet points, were prepared for academic battle. In truth, the students were respectful, inquisitive and engaged. If there is one thing that folks working in human rights rarely get, it is engagement from their audience. Ordinarily, when I talked to people about injustice, human rights law and sociological factors that lead to suffering the common response would be sombre nodding as they waited for their turn to change the topic to something cheerier. The students who filled this room, however, actually wanted to know how human trafficking occurs, why people end up in sex work and what conditions face children who are denied an education. It was clear to me from this experience that education could be a key tool in spreading awareness and fostering change.

I have been lucky enough to provide a few more guest lectures at universities, this time in the UK. The response has always been positive. However, what I did not realise as a guest lecturer is that there is a huge difference between students who chose to attend a one-off talk and students who are timetabled to spend hours with you every week. Something I would later learn to deal with as a teacher.

A friend of mine had a very different introduction to teaching. She worked predominantly in a pastoral role. Partway through her time in this role, however, she hit a moral brick wall. It was decided that she would deliver a tutorial to students on 'fundamental British values', in order to tick the latest Ofsted box. She and I have realised how important it is to view the world through different cultural lenses and felt that 'British values' was an odd concept and 'fundamental' made it sound fairly threatening or extremist.

What are British values?

- Democracy. (Which was decided as a British value without consultation of the people, by a government whose second chamber is unelected and whose head of state is there through a birth right. Furthermore, democracy is a Greek political concept enjoyed by countless nations the world over. I'm not sure it should be seen as a 'British' value.)
- The rule of law. (Which law? We enjoy a powerful position internationally and therefore can flout rules. Many nations would not have got away with an illegal invasion of Iraq.)
- Individual liberty. (Please ignore the long history of slavery and colonisation.)
- Mutual respect for and tolerance of those with different faiths and beliefs and for those without faith. (Islamophobia and anti-Semitism have been major problems in the UK on both sides of the political divide.)

The above values are not to be sniffed at. They are all wonderful values for a nation to uphold. In the case of the UK, and almost every other nation on earth, however, I would say these values are aspirational and not currently fully in effect. It is dangerous to tell a society that they have achieved such lofty ambitions, rather than focus attention on trying to constantly improve in these areas. Furthermore, these are human values, are they not? Do we need to add the word 'British'? According to the policy issued by the government no we do not – we can simply embed these values into lessons without the need to overtly state to students that they are 'British'.

To be honest, I am fine with that. I am happy to embed a vote into a lesson, to show democracy, or for the students to follow the rules, to reinforce the rule of law, and for students and staff to respect each other, practising mutual respect and tolerance. That's all fine by me. It was also fine to my friend, whose story we are concerned with here.

At the time, however, like many other educational institutions, it was interpreted that 'fundamental British values' meant that she needed to start using more Union flags, pictures of the Queen and telling students to regurgitate the words 'fundamental British values'. This approach was taken predominantly because an Ofsted inspector might ask a student what 'fundamental British values' are, and they had better have the right answer.

She was thus provided with a PowerPoint presentation, including the use of the national anthem and a running theme of linking values to nationality. She told me that she could not face a room full of students and promote borderline nationalism. She simply did not believe that morals and values come from a person's nationality rather than their personality and character. This task, pushed her to look for work elsewhere and to pursue a position where she would be in control of the content that she shared with her students. She began applying for teaching roles. Academic freedom is vital to a teacher's integrity.

Flashback: I follow my Burmese contact who wants to show me where a mother and her three children live. We walk up several concrete steps along a narrow stairwell, with the sounds of hawker stalls and customers outside. The hot sun bears down on my neck through the slits in the brickwork that allow air to circulate. We reach the correct floor and walk along the corridor to a single, small concrete room, void of any furniture or running water. There is a single rattan mat on the floor with no pillows. The mother who lives here with her children has one bathroom, at the end of the hall, to share with other residents. The room her family are staying in has barely enough floor space for them all to sleep. They are not here during this visit because the mother is a community teacher, providing education for kids from Burma. A few tightly packed plastic bags gathered in one corner display the extent of the family's possessions. I assume it was all they could carry with them when they were forced to flee their home. I picture the lush forests they had fled from, look down at the concrete floor and perhaps, for a fleeting moment, feel a sense of their loss.

Does human rights law provide any guidance about teachers?

The ICESCR asserts that 'the material conditions of teaching staff shall be continuously improved'.[53] As a teacher in the UK, I know that we certainly have not followed this. The Economic and Social Council that oversees the implementation of the ICESCR have asserted that, in reality, the general working conditions of teachers have deteriorated and, in many countries, reached unacceptably low levels. Furthermore, the Economic and Social Council state that for educational institutions to function they require, among other things, trained teachers receiving domestically competitive salaries.[54]

The Economic and Social Council further state that those in the academic community should be free to research, discuss and teach, both in the pursuit of knowledge and ideas and to transmit such ideas and knowledge. Academic freedom should also include freely expressing opinions about the institutions in which they work and the systems of education, as well as being free to join a professional or representative academic body.[55] This should be a real cornerstone of academia as a whole – the freedom to pursue ideas and knowledge and to openly debate and discuss those ideas. Nothing is more at the core of academia than the gentle but unstoppable development of our understanding of the world and beyond, fostered through research and debate. My own opinions and ideas have been challenged by students and my knowledge deepened by discussing concepts and subjects in the staff room.

Being a teacher is not merely about transmitting knowledge and ideas, but being open to having yours challenged. This is especially true as a politics teacher. I do my best to ensure my students do not know my own political opinion because it could taint their political education if they were to try and please, or annoy, me by stating or researching certain schools of thought. When students do voice their political understandings, it helps me to stop seeing the issue from purely an academic standpoint and to gain a better insight into how people view politics and why people vote the way they do.

In 1966 UNESCO and the International Labour Organisation (ILO) produced a document entitled *Recommendation concerning the Status of Teachers.* It reads like a poetic list of broken promises, the dream job description of any teacher. Before we briefly look at what it includes it is worth noting that it is a list of recommendations and therefore not legally binding. It recommends that class sizes allow for one-to-one attention and that teachers be granted paid study leave. Regarding a teacher's working hours, it asks that factors be taken into account such as the number of pupils, planning time, marking time, the number of different lessons, research and extracurricular activities, time to counsel students and time to consult with parents. There is also a section on teachers' pay, asserting that it should reflect the importance to society of their function and compare favourably with salaries paid in other occupations requiring similar or equivalent qualifications.[56] UNESCO has also established a body of 12 experts to monitor the teaching profession concerning, among other things, the above-referenced document.[57]

So, teachers should:

- Receive continuously improved material conditions.
- Receive domestically competitive salaries.
- Enjoy academic freedom.

Teachers could also, if recommendations are followed:

- Work with small class sizes, allowing individual attention to students.
- Enjoy carefully designed work patterns allowing for all a teacher's tasks and responsibilities to be taken into account.
- Receive a salary that is favourable when compared with other occupations requiring similar levels of qualifications.

Do teachers enjoy what they should around the world?

The ILO and UNESCO noted in a 2015 report that austerity measures and increased accountability had had an impact on the psychological well-being of teachers, resulting in some cases of burnout. Essentially what this means is that funding went down and demands went up. Teachers were asked to take up more work to make up for gaps in public financing and also to provide more documentation to justify the funding that they were receiving.

From an economic standpoint, post-financial crisis, one can see the logic. But the toll this measure took on teachers, and continues to take in some cases, is very real. The report further asserts that such austerity measures have demonstrated a continued lack of recognition of teachers as professionals, leading to a decline in teachers' status and working conditions. According to the report, teachers have also faced discrimination based upon sexuality, gender, ethnicity and immigration status, and some teachers were still struggling to join unions, or have unions recognised.

Perhaps, most concerning is that, according to the report, early childhood teachers enjoy the least recognition, appreciation and investment in their professional development,[58] despite primary education being an absolute right for children. Not only does the report argue that teachers are not supported as they should be, but that the situation is actually getting worse. Not surprisingly, in countries where teachers are paid less compared with other professions, they feel less valued by society. In a 2014 survey, only 30% of teachers in OECD nations agreed that they felt valued by society. Nations that did invest in education saw both an increase in teachers feeling valued by society and a higher proportion of high-achieving students.[59] Despite not joining the teaching profession for financial gain, many teachers may look at their salary, compare it to their workload and think 'so, that's how much my government values my work'. Long hours and low wages equal feeling undervalued.

The ILO and UNESCO report is from 2015. It is difficult to see how, when responding to the economic downturn from Covid-19, governments will not continue this economic rationale or perhaps double down and make even more drastic cuts to education budgets. An investment in the future requires a surplus in the present. Beyond that report, there are some nations and teachers who are in significant trouble.

Various media outlets have reported that Turkey's President Recep Tayyip Erdogan has dismissed thousands of teachers, suspected of supporting the organisation that was at the centre of a failed coup attempt in 2016. The country has since taken on a much more Islamic approach to education, contrary to the secularist ideals of Turkey's national hero Kemal Ataturk, and potentially undermining the safety and freedom of people not following the Sunni faith.[60] In essence, the president is removing any teachers who do not follow his ideals and preferred curriculum.

Separately, I would also like to state that people should be wary of any politician who invokes religion. Being religious is an individual choice and can be of great benefit to a person. But no politician should ever try to pretend that they are somehow the religious choice, or that supporting them means supporting your faith. This is an exploitation of people's beliefs and is all too often used to excuse horrendous behaviour. President Bolsonaro of Brazil has referred to his faith at a number of public events and called for prayer to tackle the Covid-19 pandemic deflecting blame from his handling of the crisis.[61] When President Trump was under scrutiny following race riots in the US, he posed in front of a church holding a bible. Both individuals may be religious men, but it is easy to argue that these examples were political stunts to try and convince people of their moral authority.

There are stories too of teachers, especially foreign teachers, being arrested and deported from China. Reports allege that the Chinese government is promoting a more 'patriotic' education system and that this means a crackdown on teachers who could bring outside influences or ideas into the country.[62]

Again, separately I would like to warn people against any politician or party that routinely invokes patriotism. Like religion, patriotism is seen as a virtue in itself, void of any need of explanation or justification. If a politician tries to link themselves with patriotism and convince people they are the most patriotic choice, they feel no need to justify themselves further. But this is often a cover for weak or selfish policies. Any politician who justifies ideas with statements such as 'it is the British thing to do', is really saying they cannot think of any well-argued rationale to sell their policy. Invoking patriotism is a simple sell all that rids the politician of closer scrutiny; it is dangerous and should be a red flag to voters. Academic freedom is clearly not enjoyed by teachers in Turkey or China.

Teachers' wages around the world continue to decline in real terms, as noted by the aforementioned UNESCO report. One extreme case is Zimbabwe. Numerous reports from Zimbabwe show that teachers are being paid a wage barely enough to provide an individual's sustenance, a wage that is more than ten times lower than it used to be.[63] This will force teachers to either leave the profession, leave the country or take up second jobs . This could have a devastating knock-on effect on education.

Teachers, dare I be arrogant enough to suggest, are special people. Teachers know they will not earn the same wage they could in other occupations. They know that they will work long hours, and have to constantly answer to numerous different 'powers that be'. However, the will to do something positive and the desire to help shape the future prospects of many young people is a drive beyond money or status. Even when society turns its back on teachers, teachers continue to care for our kids and their futures. This was clear to me, even when visiting children who were denied a government-funded education.

Through my work with stateless people and asylum-seekers, I would meet those who were giving the majority of their time and resources to provide an education for their kids. I was lucky enough to visit many makeshift community schools. These 'schools' had no formal recognition and were often set up in a single room that a community pooled their money together to rent. During the evenings, the room could double up as a communal dining area. Most of these schools that I visited had as English teachers adult asylum-seekers, who had a limited grasp of the English language themselves and almost no formal educational background. It was heart-breaking to see four and five-year-old eager young minds being denied the quality of education they deserved.

The teenagers suffered the most, however, as they were more aware of the difference between themselves and young people who could go to government schools or colleges. Some of the teenagers studied every day, with their own books, shared internet access and a will to learn driving them on. These dedicated youngsters wanted a chance just to sit their exams – but they could not.

Earlier in this chapter, we looked not only at what teachers should receive but also what they are recommended to receive. One consideration was class size, allowing for individual attention.

It is difficult to say how many students in a class allow for individual attention. In terms of managing, the UNESCO report unfortunately provides no numbers to go with 'manageable size'. According to *The Economist*, class sizes in China are defined as normal by the authorities if there are no more than 45 students in a class, though that goal is often missed with classes going beyond 55 students.[64] I have provided guest lectures at universities with fewer than 55 students, and those were adults who chose to attend. I have tried to manage a class of roughly 40 teenage students when other teachers have been off sick and we have needed to merge groups, a temporary last resort. The chance in such a class for individual attention is almost zero. In such large classes, students who are struggling may create their own coping mechanism, such as copying the students next to them, rather than gain any attention from an overworked teacher.

From my experience, classes of over 20 makes individual attention difficult. The ideal class size to allow for such attention would be no more than 12 students. However, this is just my experience and opinion. A study on this issue from 1995 asserted that smaller class sizes helped students, especially during the earlier stages of their educational journey.[65] Another study, from 1998, however, argued that there are no changes to

73

students' outcomes between class sizes of 15 to 30 students.[66]

A UNESCO report asserts that by 2030, 69 million teachers must be recruited to replace those leaving the profession and to allow for teachers to work with manageable class sizes.[67] If 69 million teachers are required, in part to make class sizes manageable, I think it is safe to assume that overall class sizes are currently not only too large to allow for individual attention but too large to be managed.

Finally, it was recommended that teachers have personalised work patterns to include all their tasks. From experience, I know that most teachers in the UK take a lot of marking home with them and often plan lessons over the weekend. An OECD report in 2015 summed up what I, and many other teachers, have often experienced, – that just over half of our time at work is spent not teaching but performing other tasks.[68] Teachers in Japan have reported spending 56 hours a week working, compared to the OECD average for teachers of just over 38.[69]

The hours can vary greatly, however. Teachers in Chile report working an average of just 29 hours per week, but they also have one of the highest numbers of teaching hours per year, an average of 27 hours per week.[70] This means that the average Chilean teacher is getting all their other tasks accomplished in just two hours a week. If you are a teacher residing elsewhere in the world, please take a moment to imagine all that admin disappearing and you being able to complete all non-teaching tasks in just two hours a week. You can almost feel the breeze and sunshine as you dream of such a reality.

Admin can be a huge burden on teachers. In Korea and Malaysia teachers report spending six hours every week on admin.[71] That is six hours that could be spent teaching, marking assignments or planning great lessons. Instead, that time is wrapped up in admin tasks that likely have zero impact on the students' experience in the classroom and zero positive impact on the teachers' well-being.

To sum up, we will revisit what teachers should enjoy and what it is recommended they enjoy, with our new information highlighted in bold. Teachers should:

- Receive continuously improved material conditions. **(Teachers have taken up more work, with fewer resources provided to them.)**
- Receive domestically competitive salaries. **(Salaries have declined in real terms and, in extreme cases, teachers must leave the profession or take up second jobs.)**
- Enjoy academic freedom. **(Teachers have been deported, dismissed and arrested in extreme cases.)**

Teachers could also, if recommendations are followed:

- Work with small class sizes, allowing individual attention to students. **(A global shortage of teachers shows that this is not met and, in extreme cases, teachers are expected to manage classes of over 50 students.)**
- Enjoy carefully designed work patterns allowing for all a teacher's tasks and responsibilities to be taken into account. **(This has a mixed response among OECD nations, the richest nations on earth.)**
- Receive a salary that is favourable when compared with other occupations requiring similar qualifications. **(Not even close... please see comments related to a domestically competitive salary.)**

How can we improve things for teachers? What's the plan?

The International Task Force on Teachers for Education 2030 is a global alliance of governments, NGOs and the UN. The task force has produced a strategic plan for 2018–2021 that focuses on filling teaching gaps around the world, both in terms of the number of teachers and the quality of teachers. The report asserts that it is not enough to merely attract people into the teaching profession but that keeping staff engaged is vital, and should be done via quality training, support and career development. To achieve this the task force attempts to guide teacher policies in countries and advocate for the importance of teachers and proper policies regarding teachers around the world.[72]

I see this as a vital starting point. If governments do not value or invest in teachers then we will simply walk away and find employment elsewhere. Since I began working as a teacher, I have witnessed many decent teachers leave the profession due to stress, and I have an annual argument with myself about walking away from the profession. The world does need more teachers and governments need to ensure that these teachers remain in the profession and continue to develop their skills and knowledge.

The core question, to support policies that can address these concerns, is a financial one. Recruiting teachers to fill the gaps will not be cost-free. Providing teachers with a reasonable workload means recruiting even more teachers. Providing teachers with a respectable wage means even more expenditure. And, finally, quality and ongoing training and support will cost money. The International Task Force on Teachers for

Education 2030 report only addresses funding concerns for the task force itself; no guidance is included on how governments can pay for all this. This is not an issue unique to this report – it is a question that has yet to be addressed by any of the documents I have researched. I suppose that funding is a matter of priority for each individual country, an investment for the future economy and the prosperity of a society. No doubt foreign aid and International Monetary Fund (IMF) loans can be used for education. But there is no readily available pot of money specifically to support these proposed policy changes.

From a political standpoint, there can arguably be much to gain from underfunding education. Besides the obvious boost of keeping taxes low there is a more contentious argument to underfund education. A well-educated population are more likely to scrutinise and question what they are told. Furthermore, research suggests that the higher level of education one attains the more likely one is to vote for left-leaning policies – bad news if you are a right-wing government. A YouGov survey before the 2019 UK general election showed that only 18% of those with GCSE level education or below would vote for Labour, compared to 28% educated to degree level or above. Between these two demographics, support for the Conservatives, inverse to Labour, dropped by over 20%.[73]

This potentially means that the more people the Conservative government keep away from university the more votes they pick up at the next election. Research in France has shown that support for far-right candidate Marine Le Pen is higher among those with less education.[74] Those with a university education in the US are more likely to vote Democrat than Republican[75] and this gap has allegedly widened, with Trump pushing university-educated voters further away.[76] The anti-immigrant right-wing Partij Voor de Vrijheid (PVV) in the Netherlands has a support base among the poorly educated, with little support from university-educated voters.[77]

This argument is simply the musings of a politics teacher. Certainly no government would admit that this is true. Furthermore, it may well not be true at all. But it is a possibility. Do governments, especially right-leaning ones, underfund education to quell questioning and scrutiny from the public? There is a correlation between education and voter preference, but we cannot be sure there is causation. Another common factor could be socio-economic status. Those who are more affluent are more likely to gain a tertiary education and more likely to not worry so much about personal finance, so see a slight tax rise as justifiable or are happy to see economic support extended to others.

If left-leaning or even centrist governments are scratching their heads wondering how to curtail support for far-right parties and demagogues, investing in education would be a great place to start.

My beginnings as a teacher

On my first day as a full-time teacher, I felt the way that perhaps many new teachers feel – like a charlatan! I was an English for Speakers of Other Languages (ESOL) teacher at a college in the UK. I had the qualifications, but could I teach another human being how to speak, read and write in English? I suppose I had managed to learn how to communicate in other languages when I lived abroad. How did I do that? Did I have any experiences that would help me as a teacher? I drew upon my own observations, successes and pitfalls to help my students. In short when learning a new language, in a new country, one tends to think:

- Why am I studying grammar and words that no one in the real world seems to use? (Everyone in the UK uses verb-ing but students may wait weeks, if not months before they start to study this. They may also never study using 'gonna' [going to], much to the frustration of teenage students.)
- Can we please focus on reading and writing? (It is much more satisfying to watch a new language pour onto the page in front of you than it is to hear your own struggling pronunciation quickly disappear into the ether.)
- Now that I can communicate with people, I am a little bit too proud to admit when a piece of text is completely lost on me. (I remember one time in Southeast Asia my colleague passed me a proposal and said that she would not patronise me by translating it. I shook my head disapprovingly as I pretended to understand the document, mainly due to her expression and how I thought she was expecting me to respond.)
- Why can the teacher not explain why the language is the way it is? ('Why are there irregular verbs in English?' 'Why does English have so many odd spellings?')
- I have managed to make someone laugh in a new language... success!
- Why can I discuss historical or political issues, but I still do not know the names of almost anything in my kitchen?

I imagined many of my new students would share these experiences. I started to properly plan what I was going to teach and how. I spent hours crafting and perfecting beautifully detailed lesson plans, something you can do when you have hours to kill in preparation for one or two lessons in the coming days. However, as time wore on and my full timetable came into practice I had just minutes to prepare hour-long lessons.

The more you teach, the more you become confident and familiar with your material, and the more you can rely upon your imagination and intuition to judge the feeling in a room and act accordingly. After much practice, I managed to plan decent lessons in less than 30 minutes and managed to plan acceptable lessons in ten. Over time I started to learn what it is like to teach in the UK, and I started to question why I had joined this profession. It was not long into my teaching career until my mental and physical health took a real knock and I questioned the UK's commitment to the right to education.

With all our understanding now regarding the right to education and what teachers are supposed to receive, the next question to ask is, what is the situation in the UK like?

5

British Study Restrictions, Immigrants and Burn Out

Inequality across the UK

After looking at the global situation for those missing out on the right to education, in Chapter 3, and looking at the situation for teachers in Chapter 4, we will now focus on the UK. How are we doing?

I have picked the UK because this is where I have most personal experience as a teacher. As one of the wealthiest nations on earth, the UK should set a good example for what is happening when the economic might needed to provide quality education is available. By focusing on one country, we can also go into a bit more detail and dive into the nitty-gritty.

Educational inequality is a big issue in the UK. From pre-school onwards children from lower socio-economic sectors of our society lag behind their wealthier peers.[78] In London, once a child from the most disadvantaged background reaches the age of 16, they are, on average, 12 months behind their more advantaged peers.[79] Outside of London, the situation can get even worse as regional differences start to show by the end of primary school. According to research from 2017, children in the West Midlands were over 6% less likely to attain high GCSE scores (5 at A*-C including Maths and English) compared to children in Outer London. The same research also showed that where a child was born mattered more for their success in later life than it did for their parents' generation. Regional inequality is getting worse.[80] If Boris Johnson is serious about his 'levelling up' agenda then he needs to invest in education across the country.

Further inequalities persist as only 33% of children on Free School Meals (FSM) achieve high GCSE scores compared with 61% of those who do not receive FSM. Chinese pupils fair significantly better than Black Caribbean pupils, with an attainment gap of over 30% when it comes to achieving those high GCSE scores. There is also a 10% attainment gap between the sexes, with girls outshining boys.[81] This means that if you have a Chinese daughter in Outer London who is not receiving FSM she stands a far better chance of achieving educational success compared to a Black Caribbean boy in the West Midlands who is receiving FSM.

These inequalities are set to become even greater as a result of the pandemic. Children from poorer families were disproportionally affected by the switch to remote learning as they, among other factors, may have lacked access to the necessary technology.[82] I would implore British politicians to heed the words of Jennette Arnold OBE AM, Chair of the London Assembly Educational Panel, who stated: 'Every child should be able to rise above their birth circumstances.'[83] Those circumstances seem to affect many in terms of their educational success in the UK. Unfortunately, there are those even worse off within our wealthy island nation. Some may be denied education altogether.

Is anyone in the UK denied the right to education under international law?

We covered what exactly the right to education means in Chapter 2. We can now ask, is anyone in the UK denied the right to education?

To answer this question, we need to look at something called 'immigration bail'.[84] The Immigration Act came into force two months after Royal Assent on 12th May 2016.[85] Schedule 10, one of the provisions of that Act, came into force on 15th January 2018[86] and concerns immigration bail.[87] If immigration bail is granted to a person, it must be granted subject to one or more conditions, including restricting the person's studies in the UK, resulting in them no longer being able to attend educational institutions and continue their studies.[88] It is worth keeping in mind here that the UK has ratified nine treaties guaranteeing the right to education.[89] This includes the CRC and ICESCR, both of which have made it clear that rights cannot be denied based upon an individual's immigration status.

Immigration bail may be granted to, among others:

· Persons detained or liable to be detained under the authority of an immigration officer pending his examination and pending a decision to allow, or not, the person to enter the UK without leave, or to give or refuse leave to any persons

who have arrived in the UK.[90]
- Persons detained or liable to be detained to be examined by an immigration officer for the purpose of establishing whether the leave should be cancelled.[91]
- Persons detained or liable to be detained under the authority of the Secretary of State, pending removal of the person from the UK, or to examine a person or to give or refuse a person leave to enter the UK.[92]
- Persons refused leave to enter and illegal entrants.[93]
- Persons pending deportation.[94]

Essentially, this applies to those individuals who are in a bit of legal limbo, such as asylum-seekers who are waiting for the Home Office to decide on their application to be a refugee (a wait that might last months, or even years) or an individual who may have tried to evade legal authorities and is now caught up in the system, trying to define their status. If immigration bail is granted to a person, it will be granted with conditions. Numerous conditions may be given. However, one of the conditions is as follows: 'a condition **restricting the person's** work, occupation or **studies** in the United Kingdom.'[95]

Home Office guidance asserts:

"A person does not have to be given a study condition permitting or prohibiting study. They must have at least one other condition of bail. If there is any doubt over whether study should be restricted, no study condition should be applied... Consideration must be given to whether the individual is undertaking significant exams... and what the timescale is when taking removal action into account, and therefore the impact of a study restriction."[96]

It is worth pointing out here that Home Office guidance is there to guide staff; it is not the law and thus changing it is much easier than changing the law. Also, it does not need to be applied with the same force as the law.

We know that for kids the right to education is an absolute right. There are some differences between the four nations that comprise the UK regarding the status of individuals over the age of 16 in certain circumstances. However, you are a child in the UK until you reach 18 years of age.[97]

Home Office guidance also states 'If a child can lawfully access education services until the age of 18, they must be permitted to study up to and including the final year of school in which they turn 18.'[98] Thus children will not have their right to education denied by the Immigration Act, if Home Office guidance is followed, and does not change.

By restricting access to studies, for those over 18 years of age, education will not be accessible to all, as it is supposed to be. Furthermore, the Coram and Refugee Support Network have stated many young asylum-seekers, and migrants are being granted immigration bail with a no study condition.[99] I too have heard of students disappearing from lessons only to have a colleague inform me that the Home Office has restricted their studies. This included hard-working students, who wanted to understand the language of their new home nation and may still be in a legal battle with the Home Office for a protracted length of time. This denies them potentially years of education that would have helped them to integrate and contribute to UK society.

Furthermore, regarding adult students, Home Office guidance states that adult asylum-seekers should be permitted to study, until they become appeal rights exhausted (APR), and admission to universities is a matter for the institutions. Only those due for deportation, post-APR and adult immigration offenders are recommended by the Home Office to be prohibited from studying.[100] So, in terms of the guidance, not the law, the list of who may have their study restricted is much smaller.

If implemented following Home Office guidance individuals may be denied the right to post-18 education on the basis of their immigration status. From Chapter 2 we know that immigration status is not a justified reason to deny someone education. Although the Home Office guidance is somewhat kinder than the law, it is still denying people the right to education.

Is anyone in the UK denied the right to education under European law?

If a nation signed up to international and regional law, they must adhere to both. The UK has to follow the CRC and ICESCR, as well as the ECHR. The difference is that the ECHR has more teeth, in that there is a court that can require legally binding changes, whereas the monitoring bodies that oversee the CRC and ICESCR can only make recommendations.

The UK has made three reservations concerning the right to education in the ECHR. None of these reservations concern immigration status. The reservation made at the time of signature states 'Article 2 [right to education] is accepted by the United Kingdom only so far as it is compatible with the provision of efficient instruction and training, and the avoidance of unreasonable public expenditure.'[101]

Concerning unreasonable public expenditure, and restricting

access to studies for individuals based upon their immigration status, the ECtHR has stated the following:

"A State may have legitimate reasons for curtailing the use of resource-hungry public services – such as welfare programmes, public benefits and health care – by short-term and illegal immigrants, who, as a rule, do not contribute to their funding." [However...] "education is a right that enjoys direct protection under the Convention... It is also a very particular type of public service, which not only directly benefits those using it but also serves broader societal functions. Indeed, the Court has already needed to point out that "in a democratic society, the right to education ... is indispensable to the furtherance of human rights [and] plays ... a fundamental role. Moreover, in order to achieve pluralism and thus democracy, society has an interest in the integration of minorities."[102]

The ECtHR has made it pretty clear that short-term and illegal immigrants should not be denied the right to education, although they appreciate that other public services may be curtailed. Furthermore, when it comes to education:

"In the Court's view, the State's margin of appreciation[103] in this domain increases with the level of education, in inverse proportion to the importance of that education for those concerned and for society at large. Thus, at the university level, which to this day remains optional for many people, higher fees for aliens – and indeed fees in general – seem to be commonplace and can... be considered fully justified."[104]

Essentially the ECtHR is happy to give countries more leeway when it comes to types of education that are less vital for society, making mention of foreign students paying higher university fees as an acceptable practice.

The ECtHR has also stated that deportation cannot be seen as a denial of the right to education in itself. This means that if someone is deported from a country and this happens to intervene in their education, that removal is not a denial of their right to education.[105]

In the case of *Ponomaryovi v. Bulgaria*, the applicants were born in what was then the Kazakh Soviet Socialist Republic (now the Republic of Kazakhstan). Their mother married a Bulgarian national and the family settled in Bulgaria in 1994.[106] The ECtHR asserted that the applicants should not have been required to pay fees for their secondary education when nationals did not do so, as this amounted to discrimination regarding their nationality and immigration status.[107] The ECtHR also made a relevant point regarding the age of these students:

"It was not their choice to settle in Bulgaria and pursue their education there; they came to live in the country at a very young age because their mother had married a Bulgarian national. The applicants could not realistically choose to go to another country and carry on their secondary studies there."[108]

So, if you move when you are a kid it makes no sense for a country to treat you differently when it comes to education, since it would be unreasonable to assume that a child could choose in which country they wanted to go to school.

One case published by Coram concerns an undocumented 18-year-old who had resided in the UK since the age of four and had been accepted to a higher education institution, before being granted immigration bail by the Home Office, which included a restriction on their studies blocking them from starting university.[109] Taking the ECtHR's findings in *Ponomaryovi* into account, one could easily argue it would not be realistic for this individual to choose to go to another country and continue their studies there. However, the findings of the ECtHR concern secondary education, while the case published by Coram concerns higher education where the UK has some more leeway and the individual is an adult.

According to European law, the Immigration Act does not deny the right of education to those awaiting deportation. The Immigration Act, applied in accordance with Home Office guidance, denies education on the grounds of immigration status. Adult post-APR and adult immigration offenders should not have their right to study denied.

If Home Office guidance is not implemented, however, asylum-seekers, post-APR, immigration offenders, undocumented people and care leavers who have not resolved their immigration status, may be denied the right to education. There is no mention of age in the law. This means there is no law protecting kids from being kicked out of school because of their immigration status. The protection of people under 18 is only in the guidance, not in statute. This needs to change to ensure the UK protects the absolute right of children's access to primary education.[110]

Although we may assume that no self-respecting individual would ever use the Immigration Act to deny a child their place at a primary school, we need to remember that human rights laws are there to protect us from government. This is why the international human rights law must be adhered to, and UK law looks like it needs to change in order to do so.

To help us move closer to respecting the right to education, the Home Office guidance concerning who may and may not be prohibited from studying should be made into law. The Home Office should also consider special treatment for those who moved to the UK at a young age through no choice of their own. And really no one should be denied the right to education based upon their immigration status, as shown in Chapter 2. Despite all the detail we have looked at here, these are just my legal findings. There will no doubt be a government official who would argue that legally the Immigration Act does not violate anyone's right to education. No matter what their argument, by introducing no study conditions as part of immigration bail the UK has slowly started to row back on the right to education and we do not seem to care. Why?

Flashback: I am following directions texted to me, using my hand to block out the glaring sun from my phone screen. The Southeast Asian humidity is not kind to me and so I take out my cap and place put it on to help stave off a headache. The directions lead me to a location where the Mon refugees and asylum asylum-seekers have set up a temporary home. My contact greets me and guides me for the final part of the journey. I walk into a makeshift community school, based in one room that leads off from a kitchen, where 20 children of different ages attend classes with volunteer teachers. I have come to do a needs assessment and find out what the children are lacking. Their food supplier has stated they will stop providing rice soon and they are running low on medicine. Someone has donated some art supplies to aid the children's schooling, however. As a welcome break from the sombre task of documenting their needs, I take a moment to appreciate the children's artwork and look over the paintings they have produced. Half of the children have painted images of their old home – huts amidst trees, occasionally with the addition of soldiers burning them to the ground. The other half have painted images of boats and planes heading to other countries. Many are headed to the US and a number are flying with a Union flag on them, or seen arriving next to Big Ben. I turn and state to one of the adults: 'This is where I am from.' He replies 'Yes, a lot of children want to go to the UK so they can go to school. We [adults] want to go to the UK because they respect everyone and respect human rights.' I smile and continue documenting their needs before heading back to the office.

How have we let people be denied their right to education due to their immigration status?

Why did one of the richest nations on earth allow certain immigrants to be denied access to education? Below is a political argument, supported by research and facts. So please take this with a pinch of salt as my opinion is bound to have shaped this section, despite my best efforts to purely follow the research.

The global financial crisis hit in 2008 and, in such circumstances, some people become more protectionist and may start to question giving anything away. This is when certain politicians and media outlets can capitalise on public anger and their newfound outlook, and start finding people who do not deserve 'handouts'. This all too often targets foreigners, who somehow deserve less than citizens. This is by no means a British phenomenon; I experienced this mindset in Japan and elsewhere too.

I have never really understood this concept. In my mind there seem to be two fatal flaws:

- A citizen who has hardly, if ever, paid into the system may use the system when they need to, but a foreigner who has paid considerably more into the system and wishes only to access it in time of serious need is less entitled to do so. Why?
- Citizenship laws are not perfect. This was highlighted in Chapter 3 when we looked at the fictional case of British parents giving birth in the Netherlands, as compared to Dutch parents giving birth in the UK. One child would have dual nationality while the other could be stateless, with no nationality.

Whether I agree or not with the logic, a significant proportion of citizens of any given country the world over grant themselves a sense of entitlement that outstrips foreigners. This is especially true in times of financial hardship.

I once taught a class of students, from many different corners of the globe, at an international summer school. I asked the class if their countries' media and politicians welcomed immigrants or warned citizens of the dangers of the impending arrival of immigrants. The students unanimously identified with the latter. This is of course merely an anecdote, but I would be curious to know of any nations where the media and politicians openly welcome immigrants, especially post-financial crises. We are focusing on the UK, however, in this chapter. Has the media normalised this kind of outlook?

Reporters Without Borders ranked the UK 35 out of 180 countries in their 2020 world press freedom index. This was calculated by the pooling of responses by experts to a questionnaire. 'The criteria evaluated in the questionnaire are pluralism, media independence, media environment and self-censorship, legislative framework, transparency, and the quality of the infrastructure that supports the production of news and information.'[111]

So, there are, according to Reporters Without Borders, 34 countries with a freer press than our own – including Jamaica, Costa Rica, Suriname, Namibia, Ghana, Slovakia and Lithuania. There are two kinds of patriotic responses to this kind of information:

- This is nonsense: the UK has the freest press in the world!
- We need to understand how we can change to have a freer press.

I believe firmly in the second response. If you know of things that could be better and decided to ignore them, that to me is the anthesis of respecting a country. Telling ourselves we are already perfect is not patriotism; it is merely ignorance. Anyway, this tells us that the press in the UK could be freer, so journalists may be pressured to cover certain stories or push certain agendas. It only takes a momentary glance at most British newspapers to tell which party or brand of politics they support.

Headlines blaming problems on immigrants and warning of immigrant 'invasions' has become somewhat commonplace among sections of the UK media. Around the time of writing this chapter certain people were calling a rubber dinghy, arriving in Dover, filled with 100 starving people an 'invasion'. If 100 tired people in a dinghy can be seen as a threat and labelled an invasion, we have the ineptest navy in the world – which we certainly do not. Such rhetoric should be challenged because it is simply inaccurate and harmful.

One place to gather an idea about how society has changed is to look at hate crime statistics. According to the Home Office a hate crime is:

"any criminal offence which is perceived, by the victim or any other person, to be motivated by hostility or prejudice towards someone based on a personal characteristic"[112]

Figures for hate crimes were first published in 2012. The total number of offences in 2012/13 was 42,255. By 2015/16 this had risen to 62,518. And in 2019/20 it had risen again to 105,090.[113] An increase over seven years of almost 250%.

According to Hate Crime Operational Guidance created by the College of Policing 'Crimes which target someone because of hostility towards their immigration status constitutes a recordable race hate crime.'[114] Race hate crime is the highest recorded hate crime in the UK, by some distance, making up almost three-quarters of all hate crime offences recorded in 2019/20.[115]

It would be easy to say that immigrants are used as a scapegoat by politicians, especially as the majority of immigrants cannot vote in general elections. The debate around immigration could last for a long time and indeed has dominated British political discourse for the past several years. Hate crime is rising, the UN is concerned about xenophobic rhetoric in the British media, and politicians too have been criticised by the UN for their actions during the Brexit referendum.[116]

It is irregular migrants whom I have worked with and studied the most. I worked with trafficking victims in the past and can assure you that those without proper documentation, such as asylum-seekers, refugees and stateless people, are all vulnerable to trafficking.[117] Irregular migration is migration that does not include official papers and checkpoints. Some argue there is no difference between illegal migration and irregular migration. However, a trafficking victim or a refugee cannot be held accountable for irregular means of travel and therefore it should not be classed as illegal. There are believed to be over 4,500 child trafficking victims in the UK.[118] Being angry with human traffickers and irregular migration can make sense if you are willing to do the research and find out how to help. But to get angry with the migrants themselves misses the point and essentially kicks people who are already down.

How about general attitudes? Statistics suggest that public opposition to immigration may have peaked between 2012 and 2015. Available statistics also suggest that the public's opposition to immigration was higher in the 1960s, 1970s and even 1980s. Attitudes may be softening somewhat after the EU referendum as well. When respondents were asked to name the 'most important issue' facing the nation for much of 2015 and 2016, immigration came out on top. Since the referendum, fewer people have mentioned it as an issue, with Europe/EU, the NHS and the economy mentioned by more people.[119] Despite the negative concerns listed before, there may be room for cautious optimism.

Is there truth behind people's concerns? Do immigrants damage the economy? A House of Commons briefing paper from 2017, entitled 'Statistics on migrants and benefits', stated that non-UK-nationals were not more likely to receive out of work benefits than UK nationals. The overall net fiscal impact of migrants paying taxes and claiming benefits seems somewhat harder to determine. That is, perhaps, the core question; do immigrants take more out than they put into the system? The paper states there is either a small positive or negative net impact.[120]

Different findings were published in a comprehensive study by Dustmann and Frattini in 2014. This study outlined how immigrants have consistently paid more in than they have taken out, especially post-2000. The paper concludes that immigrants are paying so much more in than they take out that they are in effect reducing the economic burden of public services for nationals. British people contribute less to the net fiscal well-being of the country than immigrants. They estimate that immigrants saved UK taxpayers just under £24 billion between 2001 and 2011.[121] The contrast between reality and public perception when it comes to immigrants is sadly something that I am sure will resonate with readers living outside the UK too. Immigrants are an easy target; they are easily identifiable as the 'other' and a scapegoat that rarely gets the right to vote. In the UK, however, their presence adds to the public purse, which could fund education.

With all these findings in mind, it is easy to see why there was no uproar when the Immigration Act allowed for certain migrants to have their access to education denied, especially as it would only be in very particular cases if Home Office guidance was followed. Imagine how the media and public would react if British people could have their access to education restricted. Would it still come into force with barely a whimper of public concern? The creation of the 'other' who does not deserve the same as 'us' can often be an easy starting point to row back on human rights.

Do teachers enjoy what they should in the UK?

As a result of the government's reaction to the financial crash, education has been hit hard by funding cuts. The Institute for Fiscal Studies asserted in 2017 that, despite increases in spending on early years provision, 'spending per pupil in sixth forms and further education (FE) is set to be no higher at all than it was in 1990'.[122] As a result, many teachers are working well over their contracted hours. According to the University and College Union (UCU), in 2016 FE teachers were working the equivalent of two days unpaid every week, and a teacher on a 0.5 hour contract (contracted to work half the hours of full-time staff) was working on average just under 30 hours per week.[123] The Department for Education's own research in 2019 made it clear that teachers in the UK average over 49 hour work weeks.[124] Keep in mind that it is illegal to work more than 48 hours a week in the UK, apart from a few exceptions. This currently does not include those working in education.[125]

The hours worked by teachers break the UK's own laws on workloads. This has been fuelled, in part, due to underfunding, clearly going against the international law asserting that teachers should receive continually improving material conditions.

Almost 1.5% of teachers surveyed by the UCU working in FE asserted that they work over 90 hours per week.[126] I remember sitting around the table with my family once and we got onto the subject of work. My brother asked me how many hours I worked on average and I replied 'about 45 a week'. 'Why is it 45 hours!?' he replied somewhat perplexed, and with concern. Not realising he was implying that it was too high, I replied as I expect most teachers do who work 45 hours per week. I somewhat shyly admitted that I only worked 45 hours a week because I had taken a pay cut to reduce my workload.

Do teachers in the UK enjoy carefully designed work patterns allowing for all of a teacher's tasks and responsibilities to be taken into account? This is something we covered in the previous chapter. We should look at this in three separate groups – primary teachers, secondary teachers and teachers in FE. Primary teachers teach for 47% of their working hours. Secondary teachers teach for 42% of their working hours.[127] Teachers in FE teach for just 26.5% of their working hours. However, when we add in student consultations and giving personal tutorials to students, this goes up to 46.2% of their working hours.[128] Studies have shown that a 40-hour work week is the maximum ideal for the balance of productivity and health for a full-time employee; anything above 48 hours per week can start to have consequences for health and well-being.[129]

If primary school teachers teach for 42% of their working hours, to work for 40 hours per week, they should be teaching just under 19 hours per week. They actually teach, on average 22.9 hours and work over 48 hours per week. Secondary school teachers do not fare much better as they should be teaching just under 17 hours per week but actually teach just under 20 hours and also work over 48 hours per week.[130] Teachers in FE, in order to work 40 hours a week should be teaching 18 and a half hours per week, but actually teach just under 24 and also work over 48 hours per week.[131]

If you are a teacher in the UK and you are reading this, please remember to breathe. Forty-eight hours a week should be seen as a breaking point, an absolute limit. However, all three of these categories are working over 48 hours per week. Either teachers' teaching hours need to be greatly reduced or their capacity to teach for such long hours needs to be accommodated by removing other tasks. Teachers in FE state that almost 10% of their time is taken up with admin.[132]

Despite 40 hours of work per week allowing for a healthy balance, only just over 16% of FE teachers surveyed stated that they work 40 hours or less per week, yet this should be the norm. Teachers in higher education also reported working on average in excess of 50 hours per week, with just over 1% of respondents stating they work over 90 hours per week, and just under 13% working 40 hours or less.[133] Only 9% of primary and secondary school teachers reported working 40 hours or less, with 16% reporting that they work over 60 hours per week.[134]

I have worked in many educational establishments in the UK since 2010 and can confirm that the above statistics reflect the reality. Teachers, however, love to teach. No one gets into teaching for the money or the working conditions. They are there through passion. It is a noble profession, I am proud to be a teacher, as are countless colleagues of mine, past and present.

However, burnout is a very real problem in education and I have known numerous colleagues to disappear for long periods due to stress. I have also seen some excellent tutors who inspire students and provide quality pastoral care cry in the office, from stress and a lack of sleep. There are many wonderful teachers in the UK working in other professions because they were driven away. Some of the very best teachers in the UK may be serving you your meal, helping you with your insurance or fixing your car, instead of educating your kids, because they were forced out of the classroom by intolerable working conditions.

What about pay? Teachers should get a domestically competitive salary. In the UK a newly qualified teacher receives £24,373; the average starting salary for a graduate is likely to be lower, depending upon the sector. Good news, right? However, teachers' wages have stagnated as pay rises have essentially been frozen for roughly ten years. A 1% pay rise is, in reality, a pay cut when inflation is taken into account. This means that experienced teachers are seeing no real pay increase, and watching their peers in other sectors earn more whilst working less. When 25,000 teachers were surveyed two-thirds of them stated that they had considered leaving the profession due to pay.[135] When we take into account teachers working on average over 49 hours per week that means teachers are roughly receiving an hourly wage of £10, which is above the minimum wage. However, other graduate jobs are likely to provide a higher hourly wage.

Prime Minister Boris Johnson promised pay rises for teachers, as a 'thank you' post the first Covid-19 lockdown. This pay rise, however, may have been too little too late for some. After the second wave of Covid, teachers were given a pay freeze, not even the 1% rise any more. It seems that the doubling down on underfunding of education has already begun.

Teachers in the UK are clearly overworked and underpaid. Tackling the issue of being overworked is just as serious as the issue of poor pay. Addressing one and not the other will reduce the number of teachers quitting the profession but is still not good enough. Keeping experienced teachers should be a focus, as should reducing teachers' workloads, and providing respectable pay rises.

The final issue to look at is academic freedom. Are teachers in the UK free to discuss, debate and explore ideas and research?

According to Policy Exchange, a right-wing think tank, there is a growing concern following the Brexit vote with regard to academic freedom in universities. Surveyed pro-Remain academics stated they would discriminate against a leaver for a job, and pro-Leave academics reported not feeling comfortable expressing their opinions. The report also showed that self-identifying right-wing academics would prefer to hire a pro-Leave candidate rather than a Corbyn-supporting candidate.[136]

The Brexit vote has greatly divided the UK and has become the most contentious topic I teach my students. Students will very quickly reveal to me which way they voted without saying it directly. However, when pressed on issues, both pro-Remain and pro-Leave students often struggle to back up a claim or rationally answer challenging questions. This is a sign that the debate is less rational than emotional, and possibly tribal, and people are labelling others, a dangerous road to go down. Evidence of university peers viewing and treating one another so differently based upon one political issue is a concern and may restrict academic freedom in higher education, as someone could feel less welcome or supported to publish research contrary to their peers' views. While the government, the duty bearer of human rights, has not prevented any academics from publishing or researching certain areas, some argued that it could do more to protect academics from unfair bias within institutions. This concern may have led to a new bill that was announced in May 2021 with the intent to 'strengthen the legal duties on higher education providers in England to protect freedom of speech on campuses up and down the country, for students, academics and visiting speakers.'[137] The government argues that this bill not only extends legal duties to secure freedom of speech and academic freedom but also places a duty upon higher education providers to actively promote such values. If it delivers as promised then it should indeed be welcome.

To sum up, though teachers should be accorded the rights that the UK government has promised to uphold:

- Material conditions have *not* continuously improved.
- Wages are *not* domestically competitive beyond the first few years of employment, or when an hourly wage is taken into account.
- Carefully planned timetables allowing for all duties to be taken into account are *not* in use; teachers in the UK are overworked.

If this is the case in one of the wealthiest nations on earth, it paints a pretty grim picture for the right to education globally. What is the worst that can happen? What are the ills that we are trying to avoid by providing education? We can examine this by looking at life for those who have it toughest. We shall look at some of the kids who survive the cruellest this world can offer. The next chapter will not be an easy read. It is written, after all, by someone with years of experience working in anti-child trafficking. But it is necessary to help us understand how to change such circumstances and highlight the importance of education.

6

Statelessness, Trafficking and How We Can Help

This chapter is not going to be easy to read. In this chapter we shall look at how bad things can get for kids when they do not have an equal start in life.

When we do not have education to provide us with facts about the world and the thinking tools to try to create change, societal ills can flourish. Some evils in this world will always persist. But it is up to those who value human dignity, armed with relevant knowledge, to champion the resistance. For example, racism can be challenged and suppressed but, until some evolutionary intervention, it may always play a role in society and forever require awareness and vigilance to blunt its attack.

From my experience, the most difficult starting point in life for someone is statelessness. This is where an individual may be denied countless other rights, after not being granted the right to a nationality or having that right removed. This is where we will start. We shall later move onto the issue of trafficking, before looking at the role that education could play.

Note: This chapter will involve more flashbacks and the content may disturb some readers.

What is statelessness and how does it happen?

Someone is stateless when they are not recognised as a national by any country – they are not British, Kenyan, Cambodian or any other legally recognised nationality. They have no legal home country. This person will not hold a passport for any nation. They will not be recognised as a citizen by any government. And they will likely be treated as an illegal migrant in their home. These people rarely have access to basics such as education and healthcare. Although many nations will allow the children to attend primary school, it could be dangerous for the children to do so, as they or their parents could face arrest on the journey to and from school.

When teaching students about statelessness, one common misconception is that this only happens in a handful of countries and that it is due to certain governments refusing to recognise people. Statelessness is a global issue, and each nation has its own response to tackling the problem. Statelessness primarily occurs in one of three ways.

The first is due to the conflict between the two most common ways on the planet of determining citizenship, which we have looked at before. I shall briefly recap. Many nations assert that if you are born in a country you are a citizen of that country. Many other countries provide citizenship through your parents' nationality. Both seem rational until people start to migrate, as they increasingly do in the modern world. For example, if you are born in Mexico to Austrian parents, you can get both Mexican and Austrian citizenship. But if you are born in Austria to Mexican parents, you cannot get citizenship in either country. Of course, both nations will take measures to reduce statelessness and will provide some route to gain citizenship in the second scenario, depending on where you live and if you meet other set criteria. Some nations, however, will not provide clear and easy routes out of statelessness. And some families may not have the legal knowledge or financial backing to apply for citizenship.

The second way in which statelessness may occur is that a government refuses to recognise certain ethnic groups that live in the country as citizens, which is the case in Burma. I worked with many Rohingya and Karen refugees who did not hold Burmese citizenship despite numerous generations of their family having been born in the country and not holding citizenship anywhere else. These people could therefore not migrate legally because they had no paperwork. Imagine turning up at Gatwick with no documentation at all and trying to get on a plane. Add to that reality the desire to leave the country because the government were arresting members of your ethnic group and burning down the homes of everyone in your neighbourhood. This was the reality for the kids and communities I was working with. Once we take this information in, it is easy to see why these people had to succumb to people smugglers to get them out of the country.

The third way that statelessness arises is through forced displacement. Shockingly, 79.5 million people were forcibly displaced in 2019 through persecution, conflict, violence, human rights violations or events seriously disturbing public order.[138] This displacement can cause an influx of people to move from one nation to another, often through irregular means. For example, in the 1980s thousands of West Papuans fled political unrest in Indonesia and migrated across to Papua New Guinea, where they remain to this day. These individuals have lost their Indonesian citizenship; but also many do not qualify for citizenship in Papua New Guinea, or cannot afford the costs associated with the process.[139]

How does this contribute to human trafficking?

To understand this problem we need to know the difference between people smugglers and human traffickers. People smuggling is essentially providing a service to get someone from country A to country B without being spotted by the authorities. People smugglers will likely charge a fee, help you cross the border, perhaps provide you with some contacts in your new country to help you get settled and avoid detection from the authorities – but then essentially will leave you be. People smugglers are certainly breaking the law but, given the circumstances, for some people, they may provide a vital and morally just service. Could we really state that those who helped Jewish people flee Hitler's Germany had no moral authority to do so?

Human traffickers, on the other hand, have no such moral justification. Human traffickers provide a similar service at the outset – but then they do not let people go. They will force people into a life of exploitation. Human traffickers know that those who seek out people smugglers are desperate, hold little to no documentation or legal protection and can be easily taken advantage of.

Flashback: I am sitting across from a contact of mine
in the Karen community, who had become a friend. He
offered me a cup of coffee whilst explaining to me how he
and the others made the journey out of Burma. 'We did
not want to leave our home. After the army burned down
our village, we built new shelters and moved onto a new
patch of land. But the army came back and this time they
threatened to take away my son, to force him into the
army. And then I knew we needed to leave. We walked
day and night until we reached the border with Thailand
and there we met our contact who would help us to leave
Burma. He placed us inside a hidden compartment of his
vehicle, pushing people in, on top of each other until no
more people could fit. We stayed in the vehicle for days,
with only brief stops for food and sleep. Before we reached
the next country, we needed to exit the vehicle and finish
the journey on foot. We were all told to strip naked, at
gunpoint, to ensure no bright or reflective clothing gave us
away. Once we reached the border and thought we could
start our new lives, the guns were aimed at us all again.
We were forced to lie face down in the mud, naked, with
guns aimed at our heads. We were handed a phone and
told to place a call. If someone picked up the phone and
promised to pay for our safe arrival we were placed into
another vehicle. If no one picked up the phone there were
three options. If you were too old or weak to be deemed
useful you were shot and killed. If you were a young,
strong man you were sold to a fishery or plantation. If
you were a young attractive woman you were sold to a

brothel.' I took a deep breath, and looked into my friend's distant eyes. We both knew what question I needed to ask. Yet I knew he would not talk about it until I dared ask it. I wait for the air to lift slightly before opening my mouth: 'Did all of this happen to the children too?' The weight of the question, despite being inevitable given my job, sat between us as though it were pinning down the coffee table. My question was asking if the sweet little primary school age kids in the next room, playing with a ball and giggling, were, only months ago, face down and naked in the mud with a gun to their heads. Were some of their friends shot in front of them? Were some of their former playmates now in brothels or plantations, perhaps never to be seen again? My friend lifted his head and, without being able to look at me, nodded and whispered 'yes'.[140]

All this can lead to people, including children, being trafficked. But what happens to those caught up as trafficking victims?

What is life like for a trafficked person?

According to the Trafficking in Persons Report 2020 traffickers can 'isolate and threaten victims, induce exhaustion, and interfere with their believed or real ability to escape'.[141] This essentially means the use of control and torture. I have had the extreme displeasure of having methods of control and torture explained to me by experts in trafficking, and former victims. While detailing them here would be gory, and serve no purpose in helping us to understand life for a trafficking victim, the means by which a trafficking victim's ability to escape can be interfered with includes in some cases the use of locked doors and guards.

Alternatively, a victim's belief in escape can be deeply damaged by the trafficker explaining to them that they are an illegal immigrant and will face years in prison if they go to the police or are discovered to be in the country. This psychological warfare can be ramped up by falsely promising the victim that they will be released by the traffickers much sooner than they would be let out of jail if they were to escape and get caught. Methods to keep victims in servitude could involve debt bondage. The trafficker tells a victim they owe the trafficker financially for helping them to leave their former country and the victim must work to pay back that debt, at which point they will be free. The promise of freedom is of course rarely, if ever, upheld. And further debt will be incurred for shelter and food, at a rate impossible to work off.

The type of acts committed by human traffickers would make the stomach of a healthy person turn and the blood of the righteous boil. People who cave in to their unhealthy and dark desires involving children will make the most of the services offered by child traffickers. Such people living in nations with a well-funded and organised law enforcement structure may take a trip to another country, or even permanently move to another country, to exploit trafficked children. This could involve paying to sexually abuse a child and, according to the Trafficking in Persons Report 2020, a new online phenomenon has taken hold:

"Some countries are attractive destinations for perpetrators who take advantage of weak rule of law, poverty, or the opportunity to engage in 'voluntourism'. A relatively new form of extraterritorial commercial child sexual exploitation and abuse involves the use of livestreaming, chat, and payment platforms.

Perpetrators send an electronic payment to a person in another country who then livestreams the sexual abuse of a child in that country back to the 'customer.'"[142]

Life for victims of trafficking is akin to that of slavery. So long as you are awake and able to work you shall. If anything prevents you from working, minimum care will be provided until you are fit to work again. Or else you may be sold to someone else or even killed.

> **Flashback:** *My colleagues and I are driving from our youth centre towards a meeting elsewhere in the city. Endless concrete structures pass by the windows, with the dimming setting sunlight providing a serene evening backdrop. As we are en route, my colleague and close friend points out the window to one of the nondescript buildings and states 'We have good reason to believe that seven-year-olds are being held in that brothel.' I exhale forcefully, allowing a small drop of anger to come out in front of my friends, as the implications of that statement sink in. Information such as this would increasingly become part of my life as time went on. I knew such places existed in the world, but to have a trusted friend point one out was another matter. The remainder of the journey is a blank to me now. I am sure we continued discussions and preparation for the meeting we were heading to, but the memory of that building and the horrors that lie within sit front and centre in my waking nightmares.*

I believe that further detail is not required beyond what has been stated. We get the picture, and need to digest this difficult information. Life for trafficking victims is, in essence:

- A life of constant threat and fear, where one is coerced to act as a slave.
- Full of false promises of freedom and often false threats of arrest and imprisonment from authorities.
- An existence where one is viewed as a commodity, who can be bought or sold and disposed of if unprofitable.
- No kinder to children than adults.

How big is the issue of trafficking?

The number of identified trafficking victims worldwide has increased in recent years from 44,758 in 2013 to 118,932 in 2019.[143] This may in part be a reflection, however, of improved identification and the passing of new legislation in various countries aiding the efforts to free victims.

We can focus on a couple of countries to give us an idea of how trafficking varies across the globe. We will start by looking at my home country, and one of the countries we have focused on in this book, the UK.

The Trafficking in Persons Report 2020 began its examination of the UK with praise, stating that minimum standards to eliminate trafficking have been fully met and that the government showed serious and sustained efforts. The report does, however, also state that the UK needed to provide more attention and resources to protection services for child victims and that 'long-term care and reintegration support for victims remained inadequate'.[144]

There are up to 13,000 potential trafficking victims in the UK, and nearly half of those identified are children. Labour trafficking is the most common form of exploitation with victims working in areas such as cannabis cultivation, nail salons, fishing boats and car washes. Youth victims, who have been trafficked by gangs may be used to then act as drug couriers. Women and young girls from eastern Europe are cited as being vulnerable to sex trafficking in Northern Ireland. The report also states that 'Children in the care system and unaccompanied migrant children are particularly at risk of trafficking.' Removing the stigma, and offering the needed support to migrant children in the UK, could play a vital role in freeing them from the clutches of traffickers.[145] A robust and fact-based debate about migration policy should be welcome in a democracy. However, no matter how strongly one feels about migration, blame or stigma should not be placed upon the migrants themselves.

If we move to a nation with very different financial resources, a nation where trafficking has taken grater hold, we can gain a better picture of the degree to which trafficking varies across the globe.

According to a US State Department report, in Eritrea, individuals trying to flee the nation due to its abhorrent human rights abuses, including 'arbitrary arrest and detention, lack of due process, and religious persecution', are subject to the whims of people smugglers and human traffickers.[146] Individuals in Eritrea are obliged to complete national service, supposedly for a period of 18 months. However, once conscripted, individuals may be subject to threats of detention, torture and family reprisals unless they serve indefinitely. Those who have fled, and then been returned, have reportedly disappeared, presumed imprisoned. Those who do flee may be trafficked into forced labour or sex work in Sudan, Ethiopia and Libya.[147]

The number of individuals assigned such a fate is not stated in the Department of State report. Research elsewhere appears to be lacking in specifics in this regard too. Knowing the abuses faced in their own nation, countless individuals will no doubt seek to leave, and with safe and legal routes lacking, their options are to reach out to people smugglers or human traffickers. As we have explored before, knowing the difference between the two from the offset is an almost impossible task for those wishing to flee. They are forced to flip the coin of chance promising freedom. If it were to land on heads, they shall go with the people smugglers and possibly arrive in a new country via a dangerous journey. If it lands on tails, they are to be sold into a life of servitude. If they do not flip that coin, they await the brutal judgement of a nation that abuses its own.

What exactly do we mean when we refer to people fleeing nations that abuse human rights?

I am dismayed when I hear some people in the UK say that they are 'against human rights'. It has, in some circles, become the norm to complain about human rights. Some people in the UK have also said that the UK should leave the ECHR. Some argue that a British Bill of Rights would be better because then *we* could decide *our* own rights. Please do not be fooled that *we* and *our* in this sense means me and you. You will continue to have no say over your rights. *We* and *our* in this sense means

Westminster. And if we recall what we learned before about human rights, they are in place to be upheld and respected by governments, to stop governments from abusing those who live under their jurisdiction. So, handing over more control to the UK government will simply make it much easier for those rights to be curtailed or abused, with no oversight in place. I fear that some citizens in democracies, who have enjoyed human rights their whole lives, do not realise, or have forgotten, that peace and respect for human rights are temporal and fragile. We should defend our rights, not try to destroy their safeguards from within.

If you still do not agree with me, I will set you a simple test I have set students in the past. Please read the ECHR – and decide which of those rights you want to lose.

I have worked with those fleeing nations that do not respect human rights. I have worked with some wonderful young people fleeing Afghanistan, where they witnessed women beaten in the street because of the colour of their shoes. I worked with amazing young people from Eritrea, Kurdistan and Sudan all fleeing conflict and poverty. These students have shown a devotion, loyalty, appreciation and love for the UK that I have rarely witnessed in a young British student. Having lived under regimes that abuse human rights, they know how much it means, and are thankful to live under a government that respects their rights.

When working with children fleeing Burma, I discovered that they had witnessed and survived the most horrific abuses, which no child should have to experience. These children had seen the Burmese military come into their villages, fight children, kill children, force other children to kill their parents, and forcibly enlist others into the military. Some children were raped. And finally, their villages were burned down so nothing was left. This is what life can be like when human rights are not protected and the powerful face no oversight.

Flashback: I am talking to a woman, via a translator, who can barely meet my gaze as we speak. She wants me to share her story with the outside world, so long as her name is not mentioned. Despite fleeing Burma, she still fears reprisal for speaking about the military. Her words cause no echo in the confined space we sit in, as her gentle and quiet tone betray the harsh reality of her experience. By contrast, the translator looks me in the eye and confidently relays her tale. She wishes to highlight at the start of our discussion just how beautiful her village was, how happy she was and how much she wishes she could have stayed. She paints a picture of peaceful and respectful neighbours sharing bamboo structures surrounded by the majesty of the Burmese forests and their lush green flora. She then explains how all the huts in the village had trap doors with cramped spaces below, for people to hide in. The first time the military came to her village she and her entire family compressed themselves into the small, hot space below the hut, one family member piled on top of the other. The family would stay there for hours, sometimes days, to ensure the military had gone and it was safe to come out again. She and her family emerged each time to find their cooking equipment punctured with holes, making cooking a meal impossible. They would also see fewer of their neighbours and friends the next morning when greeting the village. Some of the buildings had been burned *down and destroyed. Usually, churches and schools were targeted. One day, she and her family realised that, after seeing the charred remains of much of the village and villagers, they had been lucky to escape death. The family set off into the forests, heading for Thailand. Her tone shifts throughout her description, from joyful memories of her village life to toneless illustrations of its demise. It is clear that she is holding back emotion, to complete her story. A tear rolls down her cheek as she whispers the final words of her tale, almost with a sense of guilt and yet acceptance that it was not her choice. When her family were en route to leave the country, it became evident that they could not all afford the journey. Her parents paid for her to escape – and they stayed behind and accepted their fate. The confined room, with me, the translator and her inside, became awash with silence at the end of her story. There were no possible words of comfort. I could only assure her that I would try my best to make sure her words would be read by others.*

Thank you for reading her story.

We have to keep in mind that all I have documented in this chapter is from those lucky enough to escape. The fates of those who do not escape abusive regimes is that they are subject to rape, torture, murder and life imprisonment – often due to some personal characteristic over which they have no control. Those I worked with who had fled Burma were treated abhorrently, due to being Muslim, Christian or a member of a certain ethnic group. Those who do not escape will, sadly, never have their stories shared.

What can be done?

I mentioned in Chapter 5 how being angry with human trafficking and irregular migration could make sense so long as one was educated and wanted to help. Here is how we can do that.

Tackle human rights abuses and poverty

When people face abuse from their government, they will seek change. We have already looked at some human rights abuses and why people flee. How is this linked to poverty? When it comes to poverty, this will exacerbate existing issues, or result in abuses of social rights – such as the right to health, adequate housing, education, food and safe water. Political and civil rights can also be affected by poverty. For example, the right to a fair trial, political participation and security of the person all require government funds to ensure they are upheld.[148]

If change appears possible via an election, or even some form of democratically aligned coup, then the people may join this movement. When there is no such hope of change on the horizon people become desperate for safety, especially for their children. Commonly, families will put all their money towards sending children to another country. I worked with many such wonderful young children, whose parents could not afford to travel with them when they fled human rights abuses.

Investment in education is linked to a more inclusive and democratic society, which could aid the transition of nations towards more democratic values or tolerance and respect for human rights. If such education were to also include the teaching of human rights then the future leaders of that nation may embrace gradual change. A better-educated populace is also likely to bring a more dynamic economy, allowing for more investment in social rights such as housing and a welfare state.

Provide more education on the issue of trafficking, for both the vulnerable and the privileged

Education programmes helping people to recognise the signs of trafficking have been tried with those communities that are vulnerable. For example, 'if someone offers you a dream job in another country, how could you check this was a genuine offer?' 'If someone promises to take your child to a school for the gifted that is in another town, who could go with the child to ensure their safety?' This could better prepare those who are vulnerable to see the signs and avoid being tricked, or knowing where to turn if they suspect someone is a trafficker.

Education for those of us who may never be vulnerable to trafficking is also vital. People need to be aware that statelessness exists and that it is a contributing factor. People should be aware that strict migration laws result in more people needing the assistance of smugglers, and possibly traffickers, to cross borders. We should all be aware that nations that abuse their own people exist and that many are desperate to flee.

When I teach lessons on human rights abuses, statelessness and human trafficking many of my students appear shocked and saddened. The end of such lessons is always greeted with the same response from students, asking why they had never studied these things before. A sense of global awareness seems welcome in classrooms and could also help students in more privileged nations to address global issues or have greater empathy and an understanding of the issues that face those who are less fortunate.

Provide safe routes of travel

If people fleeing dangerous situations know that there are safe and secure routes to flee, they are likely to access them. By cutting off, or restricting, safe passages we are simply driving more business towards the people smugglers and traffickers. The UNHCR asserted in 2017 that safe pathways into Europe were far too few to offer a viable alternative to the dangerous, yet more plentiful, routes offered by smugglers and traffickers.[149]

Welcome irregular migrants and keep them safe

Irregular migrants are individuals who arrive in a new nation without documentation, or without passing the official border checkpoints. I do not refer to them as illegal migrants because if they have a successful asylum claim then no legal action can be taken against them for entering a new nation via irregular means. The former trafficking victims that I worked with were forced to flee via irregular means; no safe passage was available to them. In the case of the people, I worked with, this lack of safe passage was primarily due to their not having a passport, having been denied citizenship in their home nation. Irregular migrants are at high risk. We should not add stigma to their difficult situation, but instead acknowledge that they are vulnerable people in our country, worthy of protection.

To sum up, we can tackle human trafficking by tackling human rights abuses and poverty, both of which can be greatly helped through investment in education. We should try to address the human rights abuse of not providing people with citizenship. If everyone had legal access to a passport then there would be fewer clients for smugglers and traffickers. If we provide education to those who are vulnerable, they can spot the signs and avoid certain dangers. If we educate ourselves more, then we too can play a role in campaigning for our government to take certain measures. If we provide more safe routes then we essentially take work away from the smugglers and traffickers. Finally, if we welcome irregular migrants and keep them safe then we protect some of the most vulnerable who may be targeted.

All this means that we would need to provide more overseas aid to nations to help them keep their obligations to human rights practices, and reduce the poverty that is also a driving force behind irregular migration. We would need to open up more visas, plane and boat journeys from poorer nations, increase the funding in education and increase the funding for programmes to shelter and protect irregular migrants.

Now imagine a politician trying to win an election in the UK, who promised to increase taxes to pay for foreign aid, education and protecting migrants, and also wanted to open more legal routes for migrants to the country from impoverished nations. Once those policy details were leaked to the British press that would be the end of their political career. Herein lies one of our key problems with challenging the ills of the world – education must come first. Any policy change or shift in political direction can only take root and flourish should the soil of public opinion be fertile.

What is life like for former trafficking victims?

Former trafficking victims face a long and difficult road back to full health, if it is ever to be reached. Some trafficking victims are, unfortunately, repatriated to their old lives and remain at high risk of being trafficked again. Some trafficking victims, although they escape their captors, do not escape the realities of the lives that made them vulnerable. They remain stateless, for example. Or they remain impoverished. Or they remain a target for their government due to their ethnicity or religion. For many a return to their homeland and the repossession of a childhood that was stolen from them is not an option. Some will remain in the country that they have been trafficked to, either through a decision reached by that nation's government to protect the individual, or through the individual's will to remain undetected, hiding from repatriation.

Flashback: My colleague and I are walking around streets that we know are home to organised crime, keeping an eye out for one another, under the glow of restaurant, hotel and massage parlour lighting. We are looking for homeless kids who cannot shelter safely from the night. After a couple of hours struggling to find any young people who will accept the food parcels, we have brought with us, my colleague suggests a location that may house some young people in need. We crawl under a gap in the wall of an abandoned building; the moonlight does not penetrate the boarded-up structure. I push up from the concrete and dust to stand, now inside. I look to my left and notice rubbish piled up high, an indication that people live here. Rats run past our feet and jump in and out of

*the discarded food wrappers. We turn around a corner
and see candlelight at the end of the hall. As we approach,
we find a teenage girl lying on a mattress surrounded by
needles, tubes and spoons. Despite her emaciation, she
is still keen to speak and accepts the parcel of food that
we offer her. My colleague tries in vain to convince her to
accept more help. But we can leave somewhat relieved
that, tonight at least, she will eat.*

How can education help?

International laws are already in place to prevent statelessness
and human trafficking. According to the CRC: 'The child shall be
registered immediately after birth and shall have the right from
birth to a name [and] the right to acquire a nationality.'[150] The
USA is the only UN member state to have not ratified this treaty.
A few nations have made a reservation regarding this article,
however, including the UAE, which asserts that nationality is an
internal matter. Kuwait makes a similar assertion.[151] We also
have the Convention on the Reduction of Statelessness, which
seeks to establish safeguards against statelessness and reduce
statelessness over time.[152] The Protocol to Prevent, Suppress
and Punish Trafficking in Persons Especially Women and Children,
whose title may be a mouthful, but sets out obligations for
nations to follow to combat trafficking in persons.[153] As I found
out when writing a paper on protecting vulnerable children in
Thailand, however, ratifying this protocol certainly does not
mean that nations will fully adhere to it.[154]

If I could wave a magic wand over this earth and make immediate changes they would be to eradicate trafficking and statelessness. Ensuring every child had the right to education would be number two on my list. I believe, however, the best way to tackle the two first issues is to fight for the guarantee of education for every child.

Educated people are more likely to work their way out of poverty and help build the economies of their nations. Educated people are more likely to scrutinise and question their governments, working towards democracy or taking part in the existing democratic process. Educated people are more likely to resist demagogues and build more inclusive societies. Educated people are more likely to be aware of the pain and suffering of others around the globe and to fight for their rights. An educated population is more likely than an ignorant one to challenge statelessness, trafficking and other abuses. One could argue that guaranteeing the right to education may not be enough; we may also need to ensure that every education includes awareness of the world's suffering and the measures needed to tackle them. This will be part of the focus of our final chapter.

We now know how bad it can get for some kids, and how education could play a big role in giving all our kids a fairer start in life. We know what the right to education means and how many people may be missing out. So, how can we change this? How can we ensure that every child has the right to education?

7

Challenging Discrimination, Conflict and Poverty.

How many are missing out on education?

In Chapter 3 we determined that a minimum of 262 million children are missing out on their right to an education. There will be some adults denied the right too, but we cannot be sure of how many. When it comes to adults denied the right to education this seemed to be an issue around discrimination, where perhaps the UN, ECtHR or other international and regional law-making bodies need to be somewhat more robust and enforce change. With children denied the right to education, we shall examine this from two perspectives: firstly, the sociological reasons of discrimination and conflict; secondly, the economic reasons of insufficient government finances and personal poverty.

There were many children I worked with who thirsted for an education, having been denied one because of discriminatory militant attacks. The military in Burma had burned down their schools and imprisoned their teachers due to their ethnicity. So we should start by looking at Burma.

What does being denied education due to discrimination and conflict look like?

The Rohingya are an ethnic group that predominantly live in Rakhine state in Burma and have been the subject of violent and discriminatory campaigns from the Burmese military. The Rohingya have had their Burmese citizenship taken from them, been denied access to universities and, in 2017, were subject to 'clearance operations' whereby the military carried out mass killing, sexual violence and arson against Rohingya communities.[155]

After 2012, and before the atrocities in 2017, the Rohingya were largely confined to 'open-air prisons' where many were taken out of education and had limited access to under-resourced schools. One study stated that 47% of Rohingya children in Rakhine state have not completed a single grade of formal education.[156]

Many of the families fled to neighbouring Bangladesh, where the official government position is that formal education in refugee camps is not permitted. However, in practice, some international aid agencies and community-based organisations, under the guidance of UNICEF, were permitted to provide education. Camps housing refugees and asylum-seekers who arrived before the 2017 atrocities were allowed a more generous and formal education programme by the Bangladeshi government, even resulting in certification upon completion, but no accreditation or method to transfer into mainstream Bangladeshi education.[157]

When educating students about people around the world who live under such terrible conditions you can see the cogs turning in their minds, putting their own problems into a fresh perspective. Education about some of the world's most poorly treated people is not easy, but it does afford a sense of perspective from which a student can value their situation better and foster an awareness of those who may be in dire need of support. We are all human, however, and should not feel guilty about feeling frustrated at our problems too. Despite spending three years working with some of the planet's most marginalised children I can still completely lose that perspective and become grumpy when I have to wait for a cup of coffee. My perspective on life can quickly dissipate if I stub my toe or try in vain to talk to a human after phoning a company and listening to an automated recording for 30 minutes or so. On one level, as a species, we have an amazing ability to empathise and realign our perception of the world. On another level, we are still capable of forgetting about the rest of the world at any one moment because we are hungry or that person in front of us in the queue is taking ten minutes to figure out how to use the card reader! We are both complex yet often simple creatures and there is no need to beat ourselves up about that.

Getting back to the Rohingya, there are two clear issues with this demographic. First, Burma needs to change its laws to allow the Rohingya to access education, to the same standard as the more fortunate ethnicities in the nation. We should be aware here that other ethnic groups, such as the Karen, are also denied education in Burma. However, for this example we will focus on the Rohingya. The second issue to address is the Bangladeshi government's refusal to allow those who have fled Burma equal access to education. This is where we can see how children forced to migrate due to conflict could continue to face difficulties in accessing education even once they have escaped.

The UN Special Rapporteur of the Human Rights Council produced a report, conveyed to the General Assembly regarding the situation of human rights in Myanmar in 2017. (Myanmar is the Burmese government's approved name for Burma.) In the report, the Special Rapporteur, Ms Yanghee Lee, encourages further efforts to improve access to school, including in Rakhine State. Ms Lee also encourages access to education for returnee children as well as education provided in more ethnic minority languages and greater access to education for children with disabilities. Ms Lee then recommends that the Burmese government, among other steps, 'Ensure access to adequate health, education and other basic services for all, particularly in Rakhine State, without discrimination.'[158] If the Special Rapporteur's encouragements and recommendations were enacted we could see equal access to education across Burma.

This, unfortunately, is where things become much more political and much more difficult. The UN cannot force countries to change their actions. There is no legally binding court that could force Burma to change its laws and there is no immediate threat to Burma if they chose to ignore the report. This is at the same time both the UN's strength and weakness. By issuing well-researched, and legally justifiable, recommendations for change they show a strong commitment to international peace and human rights through an objective and unbiased format. By not forcing nations to change they ensure that nations are happy to continue their membership and work collectively on certain issues. (When an international organisation holds too much power over national governments... Brexit).

What can be done, however, is that other nations read these reports and take their own actions or collective actions in the UN. The UN itself cannot force Burma, or another nation with similar practices, to change, but they can inform the rest of the world about what is happening. Nations can then decide how to respond. Economic sanctions can be put in place, and many such sanctions do exist around the world due to human rights abuses. Collective UN resolutions can be passed by the UN General Assembly, which is essentially a warning that the world is watching, and the world would like to see certain changes. The General Assembly did pass such a resolution on the issue of the Rohingya's human rights, reaffirming the General Secretary's call to implement changes including, among numerous others, inclusive and equal access to education.[159]

The UN Security Council have been briefed regarding the situation in Rakhine state,[160] but are yet to intervene. This is one of the stumbling blocks to bringing rogue nations into line when it comes to human rights. Two such nations, North Korea and Burma, are on China's doorstep and China has veto power in the Security Council. This is why international efforts may only go so far until China also makes strong demands upon these nations to change their ways. International embarrassment and a desire to keep other world superpowers on side may mean that China will push for some reforms in these countries, but if they push too hard then people may start to examine China's own human rights record even more closely and expect to see changes there too. The same veto power is enjoyed by the UK, the US, France and Russia. If any of these nations sees intervention as being against their own interests, they are highly likely to use that veto and prevent intervention.

Essentially, to tackle this issue, more nations around the world need to take human rights violations in other countries seriously and threaten to halt trade or raise more scrutiny in the UN, as well as open trade or lessen scrutiny for nations enacting such changes. A careful combination of stick and carrot is in play and such efforts need to be intensified and carried out more globally and systemically. This is where citizens can play a role, especially in democracies where there is greater currency in public opinion. Writing to politicians and showing that human rights issues around the globe will affect our vote, and that we value the ethics of our foreign policies, may result in an intensification of efforts among the global democratic powers.

Advocating that the UN be given greater powers to force change may result in the UN losing some of its support and consent from national powers. The UN's continued existence is vital for setting standards and goals for the globe, as well as offering diplomatic solutions and peaceful means to end disputes. The world's most powerful nations are unlikely to hand over any more sovereignty to the UN, and the UN could become defunct, if powerful nations left. A transformative move around voter behaviour may yield some serious changes, but such a goal seems almost void of a roadmap to its completion. How can we change the behaviour of countless voters without something akin to a benevolent Cambridge Analytica taking data and influencing people?

What potential solutions are there?

A UN declaration could be a good place to start. A declaration is an aspirational piece of legislation. It does not hold obligations over nations like a treaty does. A declaration could be geared towards a commitment to work collaboratively as a planet to ensure every child has access to education. This could then, in time, move towards a treaty whereby wealthier nations could reward developing nations for prioritising education without discrimination, or nations could invest more in programmes already making a difference.

There are a couple of programmes that are already making changes and are worth more investment and governmental cooperation. Firstly, since 2012 Educate a Child (EAC) has part-nered with the UNHCR in its efforts to expand the provision of primary education for refugee and internally displaced children around the world. To date they have worked together in 12 na-tions to improve the quality of teaching and learning and provide safe spaces for education to take place. The partnership between EAC and UNHCR boasts enrolling an extra 1.2 million children into primary education, and also strengthening partnerships with local ministries of education.[161]

In Syria, the partnership has funded almost 100 community centres and over 20 satellite centres promoting access to formal education for children. These centres support children, affected by conflict, to be reintegrated into mainstream education or to catch up if they have previously missed out on learning. In Pakistan, where girls' education is a core issue, the programme provides home-based girls' schools, which act as a temporary measure with the aim to fully integrate girls into mainstream education. Female teachers are also being empowered to operate their own girls' schools and, when they contribute to family income, this has played a role in shifting attitudes around girls' education.[162] If this partnership were to be expanded to even more countries, it could potentially provide safe, quality educational opportunities to millions more children.

There is also a programme from Columbia that may offer a solution to internally displaced children. A paper from 2016 asserted that 12% of Columbia's population had become displaced through conflict and schools had become sites of violence. Schools had been used to recruit child soldiers or hide militants and their weapons. Since the 1970s the 'Circulos de Aprendizaje' (Learning Circles) programme has offered a route for marginalised children back into mainstream education. Flexible timings, leaner-centred pedagogy and collaborative learning environments are located in neighbourhoods where disadvantaged students live. The programme acts as a bridge, getting students affected by conflict or other life events back into education, and has been adopted by numerous other nations.[163] As of 2019 UNICEF reported operating such centres for 1,200 children in Columbia and mentioned similar successes in neighbouring Ecuador and Venezuela.[164] If such programmes were rolled out in even more nations where learning is interrupted by conflict, and were provided with the necessary funding, we could see more children eventually get back into education after a forced break, instead of missing out entirely.

To sum up the issues here:

- Some children around the world are denied an education because of their demographic.
- This discrimination in education can continue when chil-

dren flee to another country.
- Children may also face disruption, potentially permanently so, to their education as a result of conflict.
- The UN can recommend and encourage specific changes, but not enforce them.
- National governments can use financial incentives and the UN Security Council can use the threat of military action for change.
- An expansion of the EAC and UNHCR partnership could yield results.
- An adaptation of the Learning Circles programme to more countries could also lead to positive outcomes.

What does being denied education due to poverty look like?

Two issues exist in this area. Firstly, there is the issue around national finances – the building and maintaining of schools accessible for all children may not be financially viable for a government. Secondly, there is the fact that families living in poverty may prioritise work over education and that this choice is especially harsh upon girls. If a family can afford to only send some, or one, of their children to school, they are more likely to choose the boys.

One of these issues requires more than just an economic solution. When a family must, or can, choose who to send to school it is likely the girl will miss out. The Malala Fund is doing sterling work on this issue, by connecting local advocates and providing them with much-needed funds as well as training, support and visibility.[165] Local advocates are fighting for these girls around the world, and supporting them could be a key way to change policies and cultural norms within countries. If edicts demanding change to a country or a culture come from far wealthier nations it can appear almost colonial; there can be more legitimacy to working with local advocates.

The Malala Fund has also produced copious research demonstrating clearly why it is in a nation's best interests to educate girls. This type of research is more likely to gain a response compared to the moral argument that one could perhaps more naturally and passionately make. By telling nations that it will cost them more economically to not educate girls than it will to educate them may start moving some policymakers in the right direction.[166] If governments can start to normalise girls' education, and the extra wealth created by educating girls trickles down to build the extra schools, or lessen the economic costs on families, then more girls will surely end up in education. The stigma surrounding girls' education, and the gender roles that prevent families from educating them, could disappear over time as more and more girls go to school. Changing mindsets at the local level and convincing individual families may take time – but family by family, this change will come.

We should remember that it is still very much in living memory in the UK that a family would prioritise a son's education over a daughter's. This should help us to not get lost by sitting upon a cultural high horse; but it also reminds us how swiftly change can occur.

The UN set a goal to 'Ensure inclusive and equitable quality education and promote lifelong learning opportunities for all' by 2030. That goal looks set to be missed, and fall woefully short, with over 200 million children estimated still not to be enrolled in school by 2030 – and that was before the pandemic's impact.[167] The World Bank asserts that developing nations have been making progress and enrolling more children into school. In 2014 there were 112 million more children in school compared to 2000, which is amazing progress for 14 years.[168]

Despite this cause for celebration, these children may still be missing out. If we recall, earlier in the book, we realised that the right to education means that basic learning needs are met, and a focus on literacy skills should be encouraged. However, 53% of children in middle and low-income countries cannot read and understand a short age-appropriate story by the time they finish primary school.[169] We could argue, therefore, that despite being enrolled in a school they are still denied the right to education as their basic learning needs have not been met. Quality of education is an issue to be addressed alongside enrolling more children into school.

In developing nations children from the poorest families are less likely to start school and, if they do, they are more likely to leave education early. Furthermore, the World Bank asserts that people in marginalised communities are less likely to feel the effects of changes in public spending. The cause for this could be that a community of people with a low level of education results in the areas they live in continuing their cycle of poverty. The lack of education results in the lack of high earning jobs in that location, and a lack of taxes and investment in the local area. Governments are urged to reduce the costs for enrolling children into education, and also to increase the local public spending in educationally deprived areas. This would increase accessibility and decrease the financial burdens upon financially struggling families.[170]

But we must opine that a decrease in the need for children to work is also of key importance here. If a school place becomes available and cheaper than before, it may not change the fact that without your child's wage the family would not eat. Thus, the family may continue to feel that the child's work is more important than their education. Education may be a great investment, but it will not put food on the table today. Financial support for such families or investment leading to greater employability options need to be included.

The World Bank also highlights issues around the politicisation of education. One example they provide is of a deal between a computer company and the superintendent of New York City's District 29. A $6m rigged contract was awarded due to the company being affiliated with a politically connected property developer. Sub-standard computers were issued, and students missed out on the opportunity to practise with the latest technology, advance their technical skills and complete the intended maths programmes.[171]

But it is not just political corruption that can lead to education being compromised due to politics. Education is an item of public expenditure, one that, as discussed previously in this book, has faced a reduction in funding. In the UK the cuts to education have fitted well with the narrative that the UK's economic woes, post-2008, were linked to Labour's overspending. By reducing public expenditure the Conservative Party can claim that they are to be more trusted with the nation's finances. However, in recent years the austerity policies have become less popular and encouraged some voters to look for alternative options. In the run-up to the 2019 UK general election both sides, Labour and Conservative, promised an increase in public spending, including for education. These decisions to reduce, and then increase funding were based upon winning votes and public trust, and not based upon sound financial research into how to provide the best education possible.

One key to guaranteeing the right to education is to find a way to depoliticise education. As education is a government expense this may seem impossible. However, global agreements already exist that no demographic should be denied a right to education. In nations where education is being provided but the quality is perhaps too low, and in cases where wealthy nations like the UK have continued to underfund education, is a possible answer setting a globally agreed number on the percentage of the national budget that is used for education?

At the World Education Forum 2015 in Incheon, South Korea organised by various UN bodies and attended by participants from 160 countries the Incheon Declaration was signed. The declaration calls for 15–20% of public expenditure to go on education in nations where efforts to provide access to all children are falling short.[172] There is also a UN General Assembly Resolution that asserted every economically advanced nation should work towards increasing its official development assistance (ODA) to developing countries to a minimum of 0.7% of gross national product (GNP).[173] Furthermore, 15% of this aid should go on education.[174]

Within G7 nations, the right to education is much closer to being reached and often there is just a need for a realignment of political ideals to fully realise the right. However, the number of primary school-aged children not in education, or not having their basic learning needs met in developing countries, is much higher. The need for this financial shift is to ensure the building of more classrooms in developing nations and to remove the financial barriers to education.

The declaration also calls for policies and legislation to be put in place guaranteeing 12 years of free, publicly funded quality primary and secondary education without discrimination, of which nine years shall be compulsory.[175]

The funding goal is set, the policy and legislative goal is set and, if both are met, then there is a strong chance that all children would have the right to education. But such declarations are not legally binding; they are aspirational. And the UN has asserted, as stated before, that an estimated 200 million children will still be out of education by 2030.

We have already examined how the policy and legislative goals have not been met, by looking at discrimination within education policies. If we look at financial goals, how close are we? The following list, based on data released by the World Bank, shows the range, including the highest and lowest, for the amount of national expenditure spent on education in developing nations:

- Costa Rica = 26%
- Guatemala = 24.2%
- Iran = 21.1%
- Cote d'Ivoire = 18.3%
- Paraguay = 18.1%
- Malaysia = 17.9%
- Djibouti = 13.9%
- Myanmar (Burma) = 10.4%
- Rwanda = 10.8%
- Cambodia = 8.8%
- South Sudan = 0.8%[176]

We can see that some nations are meeting the target, but that many are not. The overall statistics from the World Bank show clearly that the majority of developing nations are not hitting the upper end of the goal (20%), but that many are at 15% or above, which is the lower end of the goal set by the Incheon Declaration. It is perhaps not too surprising to see the heavy investment in education in South American countries given their strong legal support for education, discussed in Chapter 2. The lack of similar commitment in African nations is also, unfortunately, clear.

The target to provide 0.7% of GNP as aid was set by the UN General Assembly in 1970. The OECD reports, however, that in 2019, a full 49 years after the target had been set, many nations still fall well short.

Despite my previous concerns regarding the UK, it was one of the few nations that provided over 0.7% of GNP for ODA. Unfortunately, in 2020 the UK government announced it was reducing this figure to 0.5% – though also stating this would only be temporary to aid the UK's financial recovery after the pandemic. Within the OECD, Turkey, Norway, Sweden, Luxembourg and Denmark were providing 0.7%, or more, in 2019. Some of the EU's less economically advanced nations provide little over 0.1%, and the EU's economic giants of Germany and France provide only 0.6% and 0.4% respectively. Perhaps most shameful is the global economic superpower, the US, providing a measly 0.15% of GNP.[177]

Nations within the EU set common foreign policy aims and goals. If the EU truly values global education and the development of poorer nations then setting an EU standard of 0.7% could both be feasible and a means to ensure compliance with this 50-year-old UN goal. As for nations outside the EU, perhaps the UN needs to reaffirm these efforts with a new resolution. Overseas aid can also be a means of demonstrating a country's power globally. As the US seeks to reassert itself at the forefront of global politics perhaps taking a lead on ODA could be one way of flexing its economic muscle.

How much of this lacklustre development assistance is going on education? According to a UNESCO paper from 2017, after a decrease in 2011/12 due to the financial crisis, aid to education slowly began to recover. However, in 2015 it was still lower than in 2009. During this period aid to education began to decline as a priority. The total share of aid used for education fell to just 6.9% in 2015. Aid for basic education in the poorest nations also fell during this time.[178]

To sum up our conundrum in this section:

· Inclusive education is promoted by the UN, and non-discrimination in allowing access to education is a legal requirement. This is not being respected globally, however.
· 15–20% of expenditure in developing nations should be going towards education. However, many nations are falling short of this goal.
· 0.7% of gross national income from wealthier nations should be going on aid, 15% of which should be prioritised for education. Again, this is largely not being met.
· Politics has interfered with the quality of education.

Flashback: I climb an innocuous-looking concrete stair-case from the street up to a single-storey open-plan flat above a mechanics workshop. The smell of the day's heat, mixed with the fumes coming from the mechanics, fill my lungs as I venture, in trepidation, towards the dwelling to which I have been invited. Inside I expect to find maybe one or two families sharing the space, as I had become accustomed to finding when working with those living in poverty. I had been invited, in part, to provide some teacher training to the adult asylum-seekers who lived here and wanted to provide lessons for their children. As I reach the front door I am greeted by a large, muscular individual in militant attire, who albeit clearly polite is also evidently screening me for security reasons. He asks me a few questions in his native tongue and, as I do not react, he then mentions my name, to which I respond. He calls inside for my contact to come to greet me. My friend walks out of the flat and shakes my hand. He mentions something to his surly colleague, who backs off, allowing us both to enter. The space was larger than I anticipated but still no more than the space of a standard UK two- or three-bedroom flat. Inside there is a cooking area, one toilet and the rest is open space, an open space that is home to tens of children who have fled Burma without their parents. A handful of adults are caring for the 20 or more primary age school kids who call this space both home and school. These children are of different ages and the adults have managed to gather patio furniture and dividing boards to create two makeshift classrooms, one for the younger children and one for the older children. Beyond food and shelter, these people, who have fled ethnic cleansing at the hands of the Burmese military, had prioritised education. I pass out some textbooks and pens, which I have managed to source prior to my arrival, and ask the 'teachers' to join me for an English lesson. The 'teachers', of course, are also asylum-seekers who have only managed to access basic education in

Burma themselves before fleeing for their lives. They can communicate basic questions in English and the more able of them can hold short conversations. Their limited knowledge of English, the few textbooks provided by me and other aid workers, and the handfuls of paper and pens shall be all the education these children receive until some governmental, or divine, intervention.

What exactly needs to change?

The laws seem to be in place to prevent discrimination but are not enforced everywhere. Different ways to ensure their adherence should be pursued, such as greater voter awareness and engagement. Programmes aimed to help marginalised children and children affected by conflict get back into education already exist and expansion of them could be great news for countless children. The economic means to ensure greater access to education have been proposed but are being very poorly adhered to. A global reaffirming of these economic goals may be a good starting point.

In our final chapter we will look back on other portions of this book to create an ideal environment for the right to education to flourish, and take into account what we can learn from Covid's impact on education.

8

Making 1948's Dream a Reality

No more discrimination

The law is already in place for this – it is just not followed everywhere. The monitoring bodies have made it clear that the right to education should not be denied to anybody. The right to education is one that should be respected for everyone regardless of any characteristic, demographic or documentation. In a dream scenario, the Burmese government would welcome Rohingya children and other stateless children into the classroom, the UK government would welcome everyone into a classroom despite being granted immigration bail and the Iranian government would not allow certain universities to ban women from their programmes.

All these scenarios, and any other such bans on education, are already against the wishes of the monitoring bodies that nations are obliged to follow once they agree to the relevant treaty Perhaps a treaty is needed specifically for education, including in clear language, an article asserting that no one is barred from education. But then this may just be duplicating the numerous treaties that already guarantee the right to education. Perhaps the musings in the last chapter regarding an intensification of international efforts to condemn such behaviour is the best remaining option.

No more conflict

The lofty and, we should be honest, utopian goal of world peace may be too far off to conceive of as an attainable target. We could, however, explore and invest in programmes that provide education to children affected by conflict. The Educate a Child and Learning Circle programmes explored in the previous chapter could eventually be rolled out globally, ensuring that even when conflict disrupts a child's life their access to education may only be temporarily affected. With alternative options open to forcibly displaced children their right to education could be protected and could offer them a brighter future than the one that may otherwise await them.

> **Flashback:** *I am wasting a lazy Sunday lying on my bed, looking out the window at the sunset, debating with myself whether I should pop some shoes on and ask my wife if she wishes to take a stroll out in the crisp British autumn air. As the mental deliberations continue, I notice an image of one of the stateless children I used to work with pop up on my social media on my laptop. Except now she is an adult, living in another country, and she*

*holds a qualification in her hand denoting her new life
as a healthcare provider. My mind fills with memories
of trying to find a teacher for her when she was denied
access to government schooling, and even acting as a
substitute teacher on occasion. I wonder to what extent
the temporary measures we were able to provide for her
aided the creation of the better life that she has moulded.
As an educated young woman, as a healthcare provider,
she will be helping countless others.*

No more poverty

The CRC asserts that:

"States Parties shall promote and encourage international cooperation in matters relating to education, in particular with a
view to contributing to the elimination of ignorance and illiteracy throughout the world and facilitating access to scientific
and technical knowledge and modern teaching methods. In
this regard, particular account shall be taken of the needs of
developing countries."[179]

This agreement has been signed by almost every nation on
earth. The specifics for how this could be achieved have been
set out with the 0.7% GNP ODA target set in the 1970s. The
legal agreement for international cooperation is in place and
the economic goal is enshrined as a resolution.

A fresh resolution concerning the ODA target, or another

treaty concerning international cooperation, will likely yield no new results. The 0.7% GNP ODA target, however, could yield new results if it were agreed upon in a legally binding treaty. Remember, UN treaties are voluntary – no nations will be forced to sign up, but nations often want to sign up as it makes them look good and also helps to ensure that others will play by the same rules. Those nations that already provide the desired ODA could be convinced fairly easily of signing up to a treaty guaranteeing the 0.7% contribution. Other nations who are close to the 0.7% mark but just under may then raise their contributions and sign the treaty too. It would be a small increase in payments for the likes of Germany or France, but it would allow them to claim moral superiority and stay in the 'club' of nations who can justifiably state their claim as global leaders and influencers. In time, this treaty could have an optional protocol asserting that 15% of the ODA be ring-fenced for education, focusing on elementary education first. As elementary education is the only absolute right within the right to education it should be free for all children, before any significant focus is moved to secondary education and finally technical and tertiary education.

The issues of discrimination, conflict and poverty could all be addressed by the following:

- An intensification of international efforts to challenge discrimination preventing access to education.
- Greater investment in, and expansion of, the Educate a Child and Learning Circles programmes.
- Make a legally binding treaty regarding 0.7% ODA.
- Introduce a protocol to this treaty to ensure that 15% of

ODA would be for education only, starting with a focus on primary education.

What can we learn from Covid-19?

According to the UN, the pandemic has been the largest disruption to education in history, with almost 1.6 billion students affected in over 190 countries. In response to the pandemic the UN warns us that 'when education systems collapse, peace, prosperous and productive societies cannot be sustained'. Alongside a call to protect funding for education, the UN is looking at the innovative methods that have flourished since school closures became necessary. These methods and recommendations could be applied to numerous future scenarios, such as natural disasters or conflict, that might also force the closure of physical schools. Many nations have turned to online learning, however. In areas where connectivity may have been an issue, schooling has been conducted via TV, radio and the distribution of print materials. Despite these creative responses, there was still a stark divide between high- and lower-income countries. A lack of access to electricity and technology, coupled with low levels of digital literacy, impacted the learning opportunities for students in lower-income countries.[180]

Online learning may seem an obvious response to physical school closures, but research suggests that the move online should be time-limited in proportion to the age group. Research cited by the World Economic Forum asserts that older students retain 25–60% more material when learning online compared

146

to learning in class. This is due to students being able to learn at their own pace and revisit material when they are unsure. However, younger students need a more structured environment and limited distractions; thus, they are likely to benefit more from in-class learning.[181] This could suggest that funding continues to be focused on the building of physical schools for primary school students and that schools for older students could begin with national online programmes where the funds are not yet available to build sufficient schools for them. This extra investment in online learning, however, would also require connectivity issues to be addressed across such nations.

Distance learning practices impacted unfairly on students with disabilities, who could have benefited from more audio narration, sign language and simplified text.[182] I know that I am guilty of this, having made the move from classroom-based teaching to online learning so suddenly when the UK's initial lockdown was announced. Usually, I would ensure that I face a student with hearing difficulties so that they can see my mouth move, or I would provide handouts with a pastel-coloured background to make for easier reading for those who experience visual stress. Teaching assistants also provide invaluable help to students of different abilities. In the haste to move everything online, despite my employer providing guidance on how to ensure materials remain accessible, I know that the lessons I provided were not as accessible as before the pandemic. If we are to move more into online learning then this is an area we should be better prepared for.

The UN also calls for teachers to be provided with more guidance, training and resources to move online as well as more psychological support to better support students through the changes without the risk of burnout.[183] I would advocate the former beyond the current situation of responding to a pandemic, as something that teachers should be provided with as a standard. When a counsellor talks all day to folks who need to share their burdens then support should be in place for the counsellor to remain healthy. The same should apply to education professionals, who spend much of their time taking on students' concerns and supporting them through difficult experiences. We all want to provide the best for our students, but with burnout being a very real and constant threat to people working in education, more psychological support would be welcome.

Extending the right to education

Continuing from the aforementioned UN policy paper, the UN has called for the right to education to be expanded to incorporate connectivity.[184] If we expand the right to education to include internet access, this could potentially solve infrastructure issues in developing nations, where certain students may be far away from a physical school with no clear paved road or public transport system yet in place. If such remote areas were provided with better internet access, they could access online lessons, both during physical school closures and also during times when a commute may not be possible. Students in these remote areas could perhaps experience a blended learning programme where they would only need to occasionally attend the school physically. Alternatively, if education were online teachers could provide schooling to several remote villages and then travel to these villages, visiting groups of students in person on a rotating basis. I am now purely musing solutions, but we can see how connectivity might be included in the right to education to great benefit. Connectivity as a right could also address some of the inequalities seen in the UK around access to the needed technology for remote learning, mentioned in Chapter 5.

We know that the right to education is free and universal, in law if not in practice, for all children of primary school age. The aim is to progressively make secondary, and finally tertiary, education free also. It would be great if this element of the right were to be restored and for wealthy nations to take this onboard. In some economically advanced nations, this already exists, most notably in Scandinavia.[185]

There are still some very rich countries denying their citizens' free university education, such as the US and the UK. From looking at the size of these respective economies it is clearly a political choice to deny citizens free tertiary education. The US and the UK are, after all, predominantly centre-right countries that uphold freedom as a core ideal, sometimes at the expense of equality. Thus, increasing taxes on individuals to provide for public services has, in recent history, fallen out of favour. But if we can dream in this final chapter and set out our wishes for the future of the right to education then why not ask that every person in the UK be able to study for an undergraduate degree, postgraduate degree or even doctorate without the limitations of their socio-economic upbringing weighing them down? Nations are supposed to work towards this end, so I think the world should happily embrace the notion of increasingly free access to education at all levels. A better-educated populace should also provide for a more dynamic and successful economy. The investment would pay off.

In a dream world, all education would be accessible and attainable regardless of the student's documentation or financial situation.

Time to reaffirm the right to teach

As a public servant living under austerity measures in the UK, I have often felt as though my government view me as a financial burden. They seem to feel that public servants, such as teachers, nurses and police officers, do not warrant a piece of the public pie. They present an image that tax money should not be used to provide decent working conditions or a respectable wage to those who chose to serve the public. From 2012 to 2019, peak years for austerity, Members of Parliament in the UK enjoyed a pay rise of £13,730, from £65,738 to £79,468.[186] One of the reasons they have stated for providing such a great wage is that they want to ensure they attract the very best. With this rationale in mind, what does that say about the government's decision to stagnate wages for teachers?

Teachers play a vital role in the shaping of a nation's future and, without them, the right to education becomes impossible. No teacher should be under the levels of stress I have witnessed or experienced myself. I recall being so exhausted from teaching and its numerous demands and pressures, that I actually could not hold back the tears when my wife suggested I request a reduction in my hours.

The Teacher Wellbeing Index 2019 found that roughly a third of teachers in the UK worked over 51 hours per week, 72% of all educational professionals describe themselves as stressed, 78% experienced behavioural, psychological or physical symptoms as a result of their work and 71% cited workload as the main reason for considering leaving the profession.[187]   With the conditions we considered in Chapter 4 this should not be too surprising. However, what is of concern is that the UK is one of the wealthiest nations on earth and teachers are working under even worse conditions elsewhere across the globe. To the teachers in Burma risking their lives to provide education to stateless minority groups, we should all be tipping our hats. To the teachers in Turkey who dare to defy the president and put their students' education before their own safety, we again owe a debt. To teachers who offer classes to girls when the Taliban are close by, we can only look on in awe. Finally, to the teachers in Zimbabwe who risk financial ruin to aid the nation's children, we should draw inspiration.

To truly live up to the ideals of the right to education we must protect those who deliver this right. The working conditions for teachers should at least be on par with those in other sectors of society. Teachers working under extreme conditions, as touched upon above, need to be afforded some sort of recognised protection, or international support. The world should be outraged when a teacher must risk their life to help our children. Teachers deserve to be treated with dignity and to feel that the government wants to support them to complete their work, not punish them for choosing a career in public service.

Teachers are in a position of trust and, in order to provide the best education for their students, they should be qualified and held to a high standard. Teachers should continue to adhere to codes of conduct that place professional boundaries between them and their students, as well as offering their students a well-rounded and holistic education. However, when society places responsibilities upon individuals it should also support those individuals and help them to feel valued. Teachers should be working a maximum of 40 hours per week, teachers should be earning a respectable and competitive salary, and they should be free to teach anyone who comes to them. Healthy teachers made to feel valued will no doubt provide a better experience in the classroom and better education for our children.

Remembering the ideal

In the UDHR, regarding the right to education, it is asserted that:

"Education shall be directed to the full development of the human personality and to the strengthening of respect for human rights and fundamental freedoms. It shall promote understanding, tolerance and friendship among all nations, racial or religious groups, and shall further the activities of the United Nations for the maintenance of peace."[188]

In the CRC, it states that education of the child shall be directed to:

"The development of respect for human rights and fundamental freedoms, and for the principles enshrined in the Charter of the United Nations."[189]

Personally, I have found it repugnant to see far-right groups try and usurp the intentions of World War Two heroes and allied forces. We must always remember that the allied powers in World War Two fought together, through international cooperation, to destroy the idea of expansionist nationalism promoted by the Nazis.

With concern about the far-right trying to hijack World War Two in the UK, we should not forget that Caribbean, African and Indian troops played a key role in fighting for Britain, with thousands supporting the war effort.[190] We should also remember that Polish fighter pilots played a potentially pivotal role in the Battle of Britain[191] and that the Polish also made breakthroughs that paved the way for the British to unlock the Nazi's enigma codes. It was an international effort, with countless other unsung heroes.

I fear that without our education systems playing a key role in keeping such history and ideals alive we may lose them to those who wish to rewrite history in their own interests. The disastrous misinterpretation of 'fundamental British values' explained in Chapter 5 has dragged the UK's education system painfully away from the UN's original intent. These original ideals should be mandated into education systems around the world, allowing children to grow up understanding the importance of human rights and freedoms. If our knowledge of human rights and freedoms are restricted, how can we achieve our democratic duty of upholding and protecting them? These rights and freedoms were fought for and won with the highest of sacrifices. We need only to understand, enjoy and protect them. Education would be one key way to do so.

As a teacher in the UK, I know that some elements of the UN's ideal have been maintained. Teachers are supposed to embed equality and diversity into lessons, helping young people to understand different cultures and build respect and tolerance for those of different ethnic, religious or national backgrounds. When I teach students about the UN or human rights, however, it is incredibly rare for a student to inform me that they have had the chance to study this before and even rarer for a student to answer open questions at the start of a lesson when I gauge their level of understanding for a new topic.

> *Flashback: I am sitting at home, the electric heating barely warming me from the cold English winter air. As I relax after one of my first months as a full-time teacher, I check my phone and realise that I have a message from one of the kids I used to work with in Southeast Asia, now a young woman. We had helped her stay safe in a dangerous neighbourhood and we provided her space to complete her homework, as well as helping her with it when we could. She has written me a message to ask if I can help with her university project. A smile beams across my face as I realise that she has made it onto her chosen degree path. I wonder how much our educational support had helped her to build a brighter future.*

Education can be used deliberately as a tool to challenge discrimination and mistreatment around the world. Why not educate kids about the UN and human rights? Why not educate kids on statelessness? Why not educate young people on human trafficking? Why should topics that so deeply affect the lives of millions of people worldwide need to wait until an adult chooses to study them? We have focused education so much on future careers that we may be missing the bigger picture of educating the whole person and helping them to make ethical choices building a world we can be proud of.

In an ideal scenario, healthy and valued teachers around the world would welcome classes of 15–20 students to study a multitude of subjects. Children, young people and adults of all demographics would learn about the importance of their rights and freedoms, as well as learning about those who do not yet enjoy such rights. These lessons would be increasingly free after governments uphold their funding commitments and reaffirm the value of education. These educated students will create more inclusive societies, be less likely to fall for demagogues, lower crimes rates and build stronger economies. If we wish to see a world where discrimination, poverty, trafficking and statelessness are merely subjects for history lessons then surely we need to raise a citizenry ready to tackle those issues.

If the ideals are upheld then the right to education could build a better world.

Acknowledgments

First and foremost, I want to thank my wife who has put up with me spending hours researching and writing when we could have been watching a film together enjoying a bowl of popcorn.

I could not have produced a book of this standard without my editor James Ryan. I also need to thank Rebecca Collins for proofreading this work and Elisabeth Heissler for producing the book cover.

To all of my friends and family, thank you for encouraging me to write what I really wanted to. Especially my mum who listened more than most and my friend Natalie who proofread that early draft. Thank you also to Miya who spoke with me about her amazing work with EAC.

To all of the children and young people I have worked with over the years, thank you for your positive and fresh outlook on life. It always helped to remind me that adults do not have all the answers and sometimes we need to learn from you.

To all of my old colleagues in Southeast Asia, thank you so much for the great work we did together. Continue the fantastic work you do and know that I will, in some small way, continue to fight for these kids.

Finally, thank you for reading this book. If you gained something, then all the research and lost sleep was worth it.

Notes

RELIGION, NAZIS AND THE UNITED NATIONS

1   Malcolm M. Shaw, *International Law* (Cambridge: Cambridge University Press 2008).

2   Hannah Arendt, *The Origins of Totalitarianism* (Cleveland and New York: Meridian Books 1951) 293–296.

3   BBC "B&B ruling: Discrimination a right – Nick Griffin" (*BBC*, 19 October 2012) <*B&B ruling: Discrimination a right – Nick Griffin – BBC News*> accessed 28/11/2020.

4   Vienna Convention on the Law of Treaties 1969, art 26.

5   United Nations Treaty Collection, '8. Convention on the Elimination of All Forms of Discrimination against Women' (United Nations Treaty Collection) <*https://treaties.un.org/Pages/ViewDetails.aspx?src=TREATY&mtdsg_no=IV-8&chapter=4&clang=_en#EndDec*> accessed 16/12/2020.

6   The International Criminal Court, 'Kenyatta Case: ICC-01/09-02/11' (International Criminal Court) <*https://www.icc-cpi.int/kenya/kenyatta*> accessed 29/04/2021.

7   Committee on the Elimination of Racial Discrimination, 'Concluding observations on the combined twenty-first to twenty-third periodic reports of the United Kingdom of Great Britain and Northern Ireland' (3 October 2016) UN Doc CERD/C/GBR/CO/21–23.

8   *Lee (Respondent) v. Ashers Baking Co Ltd (Appellants) (Northern Ireland)* [2018] UKSC 49.

9   International Covenant on Civil and Political Rights 1966, art 4(1).

10 Ian Werrett, 'If human rights are grounded in the inherent dignity of the individual, how can derogation ever be justified?' (2015) 1(2) *Elenchus Law Review* 108, 108–126.

THE WORLD, EUROPE, AFRICA, THE AMERICAS AND ASIA

11 Hagit Lavsky, *New Beginnings: Holocaust Survivors in Bergen-Belsen and the British Zone* (Detroit, MI: Wayne State University Press 2002) 168.

12 Committee on Economic, Social and Cultural Rights, 'General Comment No. 13: The Right to Education (art 13)' (Twenty-first Session, on 8 December 1999) UN Doc E/C.12/1999/10 1.

13 Committee on Economic, Social and Cultural Rights, 'General Comment No. 13: The Right to Education (Art. 13)' (Twenty-first Session, on 8 December 1999) UN Doc E/C.12/1999/10 1.

14 Universal Declaration of Human Rights 1948, art 26.

15 International Covenant on Civil and Political Rights 1966, art 18(4).

16 Human Rights Committee, 'General Comment No. 22: The right to freedom of thought, conscience and religion (art 18)' (30 July 1993) UN Doc CCPR/C/21/Rev.1/Add.4, 6.

17 International Covenant on Economic, Social and Cultural Rights 1966, arts 13 and 14.

18 International Covenant on Economic, Social and Cultural Rights 1966, art 13.

19 Committee on Economic, Social and Cultural Rights, 'General Comment No. 13: The Right to Education' (Twenty-first Session, 8 December 1999) UN Doc E/C.12/1999/10, 13 and 14.

20 Convention on the Rights of the Child 1989, art 29

21 UNESCO, *World Declaration on Education for All and Framework for Action to Meet Basic Learning Needs,* (Jomtien, Thailand: UNESCO 1990)

22 Convention on the Elimination of All Forms of Discrimination Against Women 1979, art 10.

23 Convention on the Rights of Persons with Disabilities 2007, art 24.

24 International Convention on the Elimination of All Forms of Racial Discrimination 1965, art 7; International Convention on the Protection of the Rights of All Migrant Workers and Members of their Families 1990, arts 43 and 45; Convention Relating to the Status of Refugees 1951, art 22.

25 Convention Relating to the Status of Refugees 1951, art 22.

26 UNESCO Convention against Discrimination in Education 1960, art 1.

27 International Convention on the Protection of the Rights of All Migrant Workers and Members of their Families 1990, art 45.

28 Committee on the Rights of the Child, 'General Comment number 6 Treat ment of unaccompanied and separated children outside their country of

origin' (Thirty-ninth session 17 May–3 June 2005) UN Doc CRC/GC/2005/6, 12.

29 Convention on the Rights of the Child 1989, art 1.

30 Economic and Social Council, 'Non-discrimination in economic, social and cultural rights (art. 2, para. 2, of the International Covenant on Economic, Social and Cultural Rights)' (2 July 2009) UN Doc E/C.12/GC/20, 30.

31 Association of Southeast Asian Nations (ASEAN), 'ASEAN Human Rights Declaration and Phnom Penh Statement on the Adoption of the ASEAN Human Rights Declaration' (Phnom Penh 19 November 2012), arts 2, 4 and 31.

32 African Charter on Human and People's Rights 1981, art 17.

33 African Charter on Human and People's Rights 1981, Preamble.

34 African Commission on Human and People's Rights, '346 Resolution on the Right to Education in Africa – ACHPR/Res.346(LVIII)2016' <*https://www.ac hpr.org/sessions/resolutions?id=385*> accessed 10/12/2020.

35 American Convention on Human Rights 1969, art 26.

36 Charter of the Organisation of American States 1948, arts 34 and 47.

37 Charter of the Organisation of American States 1948, art 49.

38 European Convention on Human Rights 1950, Protocol 1, art 2.

39 European Court of Human Rights, 'Guide on Article 2 of Protocol No. 1 to the European Convention on Human Rights' (31 August 2020).

40 European Court of Human Rights, 'Guide on Article 2 of Protocol No. 1 to the European Convention on Human Rights' (31 August 2020), 9.

262 MILLION CHILDREN, LIFE-EXPECTANCY AND CRIME

41 UNICEF, *Every Child Learns education strategy 2019–2030* (New York: UNICEF 2019) 12.

42 Centre for Human Rights in Iran, 'Women's education' (Centre for Human Rights in Iran, 23 February 2015) <*https://www.iranhumanrights.org/2015/ 02/womenreport-womens-education/*> accessed 30/12/2020.

43 United Nations Department of Economic and Social Affairs, *Disability and Development Report Realizing the Sustainable Development Goals by, for and with persons with disabilities 2018* (New York: UNDESA 2019) 81–83.

44 Joe MacCarthy, 'Globally, Millions of Children in Crises Are Denied an Education' (*Global Citizen*, 17 September 2019) <https://www.globalcit

izen.org/es/content/education-in-emergencies-explainer/> accessed 30/12/2020.

45 Malala Fund, 'Girls' education' (*Malala Fund*, 2020) <*https://www.malala.or g/girls-education?gclid=EAIaIQobChMI6YS4js317QIVyJ7tCh3LTQEPEAAYASAA EgLPu_D_BwE*> accessed 30/12/2020.

46 Malala Yousafzai with Christina Lamb, *I am Malala* (London: Weidenfeld & Nicolson 2013)

47 Actionaid, 'Child marriage' (*Actionaid*, 12 November 2020) <*https://www.a ctionaid.org.uk/about-us/what-we-do/violence-against-women-and-girls/ child-marriage*> accessed 30/12/2020.

48 OECD, *Health at a Glance 2017: OECD Indicators* (Paris: OECD Publishing 2017), 50.

49 Debora MacKenzie, 'More education is what makes people live longer, not more money' (*New Scientist* 18 April 2018) <*https://www.newscientist.com/ article/2166833-more-education-is-what-makes-people-live-longer-not- more-money/*> accessed 30/12/2020.

50 Lance Lochner, '*Non-Production Benefits of Education: Crime, Health, and Good Citizenship*' (2011) Working Paper 16722 National Bureau of Economic Research Working Paper Series <*https://www.nber.org/papers/w16722*> accessed 30/12/2020, 8.

51 OECD, *Education at a Glance 2012: Highlights* (Paris: OECD Publishing 2012) 38.

52 Lance Lochner, '*Non-Production Benefits of Education: Crime, Health, and Good Citizenship*' (2011) Working Paper 16722 National Bureau of Economic Research Working Paper Series <*https://www.nber.org/papers/w16722*> accessed 30/12/2020, 61.

BROKEN PROMISES, UNDERPAID AND OVERWORKED

53 International Covenant on Economic, Social and Cultural Rights 1966, art 13(2)(e).

54 Committee on Economic, Social and Cultural Rights, 'General Comment No 13: The Right to Education' (Twenty-first Session, 8 December 1999) UN Doc E/C.12/1999/10, 6(a), 27, 50.

55 Committee on Economic, Social and Cultural Rights, 'General Comment No 13: The Right to Education' (Twenty-first Session, 8 December 1999) UN Doc E/C.12/1999/10, 13, 39.

56 UNESCO/ILO, *Recommendation concerning the Status of Teachers* (Paris: UNESCO/ILO 1966) IX, X.

57 UNESCO, 'Monitoring of international normative instruments regarding the teaching profession' (*UNESCO*) <*https://en.unesco.org/themes/teachers/ceart*> accessed 14/01/2021.

58 Joint ILO–UNESCO Committee of Experts on the Application of the Recommendations concerning Teaching Personnel, 'Final Report' (Twelfth Session, Paris, 20–24 April 2015) UN Doc CEART/12/2015/14, 3, 30.

59 Dion Burns and Linda Darling-Hammond, *Teaching Around the World: What can TALIS tell us?* (Stanford, CA: Stanford Centre for Opportunity Policy in Education 2014) 11–12.

60 AsiaNews.it, 'Erdogan's purge of schools: 2500 institutions targeted, 30 thousand teachers dismissed' (*AsiaNews.it*, 27 March 2018) <*http://www.asianews.it/news-en/Erdogan%27s-purge-of-schools:-2500-institutions-targeted,-30-thousand-teachers-dismissed-43464.html*> accessed 14/01/202; Daren Butler, 'With more Islamic schooling, Erdogan aims to reshape Turkey' (*Reuters*, 25 January 2018) <*https://www.reuters.com/investigates/special-report/turkey-erdogan-education/*> accessed 14/01/2021.

61 Dom Phillips, 'Evangelical Christians in Brazil resolve to "bring Jesus" to carnival revelers' (*The Guardian*, 26 February 2020) <https://www.theguardian.com/world/2020/feb/26/evangelical-christians-in-brazil-resolve-to-bring-jesus-to-carnival-revelers> accessed 27/03/2021; Lisandra Paraguassu, 'Brazil's Bolsonaro turns to prayer in coronavirus crisis' (*Reuters*, 4 April 2020) <https://www.reuters.com/article/us-health-coronavirus-brazil-bolsonaro-idUSKBN21L3DL'> accessed 27/03/2021.

62 Cate Cadell, 'Class dismissed: Surge in arrests of foreign teachers in China' (*Reuters*, 13 August 2019) <*https://uk.reuters.com/article/uk-china-education/class-dismissed-surge-in-arrests-of-foreign-teachers-in-china-idUKKCN1V2237*> accessed 14/01/2021.

63 Pindula News, 'ZCTU backs rural teachers' call for better pay' (*Pindula News*, 21 July 2020) <*https://news.pindula.co.zw/2020/07/21/zctu-backs-rural-teachers-call-for-better-pay/*> accessed 14/01/2021; The Economist, 'Zimbabwe's worst economic crises in more than a decade' (*The Economist*, 9 July 2020) <*https://www.economist.com/middle-east-and-africa/2020/07/09/zimbabwes-worst-economic-crisis-in-more-than-a-decade*> accessed 14/01/2021.

64 Leiyang, 'Anger grows in China over school crowding' (*The Economist*, 13

September 2018) <*https://www.economist.com/china/2018/09/13/anger-gro ws-in-china-over-school-crowding*> accessed 14/01/2021.

65 Frederick Mosteller, 'The Tennessee Study of Class Size in the Early School Grades' (1995) 5(2) The Future of Children <*http://edsource.org/wp-content/ uploads/old/STAR.pdf*> accessed 14/01/2021, 125–126.

66 Caroline M. Hoxby, 'The effects of class size and composition on student achievement: New evidence from natural population variation' (1998) National Bureau of Economic Research <*https://www.nber.org/papers/w6 869.pdf*> accessed 14/01/2021, 30.

67 International Task Force on Teachers For Education 2030, *Strategic Plan 2018–2021* <*http://www.unesco.org/new/fileadmin/MULTIMEDIA/FIELD/Bei rut/video/TF.pdf*> accessed 14/01/2021, 7.

68 OECD, 'Education indicators in focus: How much time do teachers spend on teaching and non-teaching activities' <*https://www.oecd-ilibrary.org/educa tion/how-much-time-do-teachers-spend-on-teaching-and-non-teaching- activities_5js64kndz1f3-en*>, 2–3.

69 Nippon.com, 'Japanese Teachers work longest among OECD economies' (*Nippon.com*, 9 June 2019) <*https://www.nippon.com/en/news/yjj201906 1901159/japanese-teachers-work-longest-among-oecd-economies.html*> accessed 14/01/2021.

70 OECD, 'Education indicators in focus: How much time do teachers spend on teaching and non-teaching activities' <*https://www.oecd-ilibrary.org/educa tion/how-much-time-do-teachers-spend-on-teaching-and-non-teaching- activities_5js64kndz1f3-en*>, 2–3.

71 OECD, 'Education indicators in focus: How much time do teachers spend on teaching and non-teaching activities' <*https://www.oecd-ilibrary.org/educa tion/how-much-time-do-teachers-spend-on-teaching-and-non-teaching- activities_5js64kndz1f3-en*>, 3.

72 International Task Force on Teachers For Education 2030, *Strategic Plan 2018–2021* <*http://www.unesco.org/new/fileadmin/MULTIMEDIA/FIELD/Bei rut/video/TF.pdf*> accessed 14/01/2021.

73 Chris Curtis, '2019 General Election: the demographics dividing Britain (*YouGov*, 31 October 2019) <*https://yougov.co.uk/topics/politics/articles-r eports/2019/10/31/2019-general-election-demographics-dividing-britai*> accessed 14/01/2021.

74 Joseph Rynkiewicz, Mohamed Raouf Benmakrelouf and Wafa Karouche 'Assessment of the influence of education level on voting intention for the

extreme right in France' (2015) Conference: IWOR 2015 Havana, Cuba < *https://www.researchgate.net/publication/274080022_Assessment_of_the_ influence_of_education_level_on_voting_intention_for_the_extreme_right _in_France*> accessed 14/01/2021; Statista, 'Share of votes in the French Presidential election second round of 2017, by educational level' (*Statista*) .< *https://www.statista.com/statistics/1037246/french-election-results-by-age/* > accessed 14/01/2021.

75 Pew Research Centre, 'In Changing U.S. Electorate, Race and Education Remain Stark Dividing Lines' (*Pew Research Centre*, 2 June 2020) <*https://w ww.pewresearch.org/politics/2020/06/02/in-changing-u-s-electorate-race- and-education-remain-stark-dividing-lines/*> accessed 14/01/2021.

76 Michael T. Nietzel, 'Biden Holds 21 Point Lead Among Voters With a College Degree in Six Key States' (*Forbes*, 25 June 2020) <*https://www.forbes.co m/sites/michaeltnietzel/2020/06/25/biden-holds-21-point-lead-among-t hose-with-at-least-a-college-degree-in-six-key-states/?sh=27f812f575b3*> accessed 14/01/2021.

77 Statista, 'Distribution of Partij voor de Vrijheid (PVV) voters in the Nether-lands as of 2019, by level of education' (*Statista*) <*https://www.statista.com/ statistics/807246/distribution-of-pvv-voters-in-the-netherlands-by-level- of-education/*> accessed 14/01/2021.

BRITISH STUDY RESTRICTIONS, IMMIGRANTS AND BURN OUT

78 Kate Pickett, 'Inequality of education in the UK among highest of rich nations' (*The Conversation*, 30 October 2018) <*https://theconversation.com/ inequality-of-education-in-the-uk-among-highest-of-rich-nations-10551 9*> accessed 12/05/2021.

79 London.Gov, 'Mid the Gap: Rising educational inequality for young Lon-doners' (*London.gov.uk*, 07 January 2020) <*https://www.london.gov.uk/a bout-us/london-assembly/london-assembly-publications/mind-gap-rising -educational-inequality-young-londoners#:~:text=Mind the Gap%3A Rising educational inequality for young Londoners,-Date published%3A&text=By the age of 16,behind their more advantaged peers.&text=London enrols a much higher,backgrounds than the English average.*> accessed 13/05/2021.

80 The Social Market Foundation, *Commission on Inequality in Education* (June 2017) 9, 11.

81 The Social Market Foundation, *Commission on Inequality in Education* (June 2017) 10, 13.

82 Richard Blundell et al, *Inequalities in education, skills, and incomes in the UK: The implications of the COVID-19 pandemic* (Institute for Fiscal Studies: 23 March 2021) 33.

83 London.Gov, 'Mid the Gap: Rising educational inequality for young Londoners' (*London.gov.uk*, 07 January 2020) <*https://www.london.gov.uk/about-us/london-assembly/london-assembly-publications/mind-gap-rising-educational-inequality-young-londoners#:~:text=Mind the Gap%3A Rising educational inequality for young Londoners,-Date published%3A&text=By the age of 16,behind their more advantaged peers.&text=London enrols a much higher,backgrounds than the English average.*> accessed 13/05/2021.

84 Much of the discussion that follows on the UK Immigration Act is paraphrased, or taken, from an article I had published in the *International Journal for Research in Law*: Ian Werrett, 'Does the United Kingdom's Immigration Act 2016 Deny People the Right to Education?' (2018) 3(4) International Journal for Research in Law 415.

85 Gov.UK, 'Immigration Act 2016' (*Gov.UK*, 17 September 2015, last updated 1 December 2016) <*https://www.gov.uk/government/collections/immigration-bill-2015-16*> accessed 06/08/2018.

86 Immigration Act 2016 (Commencement No. 7 and Transitional Provisions) Regulations 2017, SI 2017/1241, reg 2.

87 Immigration Act 2016, s 61.

88 Immigration Act 2016, s 61, Sch 10, para 2(1)(b).

89 International Covenant on Economic, Social and Cultural Rights 1966, art 13; Convention on the Rights of the Child 1989, art 28; Protocol to the Convention for the Protection of Human Rights and Fundamental Freedoms 1952, art 2; Convention on the Elimination of All Forms of Discrimination against Women 1979, art 10; International Convention on the Elimination of All Forms of Racial Discrimination 1966, art 5; Convention on the Rights of Persons with Disabilities 2006, art 24, International Convention on the Protection of the Rights of All Migrant Workers and Members of their Families 1990, arts 12.4, 30, 43, 45; Convention Relating to the Status of Refugees 1951, art 22; International Covenant on Civil and Political Rights 1966, art 18.

90 Immigration Act 1971 s 4, Sch 2, para 16(1).

91 Immigration Act 1971 s 4, Sch 2, para 16(1)(a).

92 Nationality, Immigration and Asylum Act 2002, s 62.

93 Immigration Act 1971 s 4, Sch 2, para 16(2).

94 Immigration Act 1971 s 5, Sch 2, para 2(1), (2) or (3).

95 Immigration Act 2016, s 61, Sch 10, para 2(1).

96 Home Office, *Immigration Bail Version 2.0* (8 May 2018) p. 13.

97 NSPCC, 'Children and the law' (*NSPCC*, 17 December 2020) <*https://www.nsp cc.org.uk/preventing-abuse/child-protection-system/legal-definition-child-rights-law/legal-definitions/*> accessed 28/01/2021.

98 Home Office, *Immigration Bail Version 2.0* (8 May 2018) p. 13.

99 Coram, Children's Legal Centre, *Immigration Bail and Studying Coram Children's Legal Centre's briefing* (March 2018) 4–5, Refugee Support Network, 'News' <*https://www.refugeesupportnetwork.org/lists/2-news*> accessed 07/08/2018.

100 Home Office, *Immigration Bail Version 2.0* (8 May 2018) p. 13.

101 Council of Europe, 'Reservations and Declarations for Treaty No.009 – Protocol to the Convention for the Protection of Human Rights and Fundamental Freedoms' (*Council of Europe*, as of 07/08/2018) <*https://www .coe.int/en/web/conventions/full-list/-/conventions/treaty/009/declarations? p_auth=HFMKSRxz&_coeconventions_WAR_coeconventionsportlet_enVigue ur=false&_coeconventions_WAR_coeconventionsportlet_searchBy=state&_co econventions_WAR_coeconventionsportlet_codePays=UK&_coeconventions_ WAR_coeconventionsportlet_codeNature=2*> accessed 07/08/2018.

102 *Ponomaryovi v. Bulgaria* App no 5335/05 (ECHR, 28 November 2011) 55.

103 'The term 'margin of appreciation' refers to the space for manoeuvre that the Strasbourg organs are willing to grant national authorities, in fulfilling their obligations under the European Convention on Human Rights'. Council of Europe, 'The Margin of Appreciation' (*Council of Europe*) <*https://www.coe .int/t/dghl/cooperation/lisbonnetwork/themis/echr/paper2_en.asp*> accessed 07/08/2018.

104 *Ponomaryovi v. Bulgaria* App no 5335/05 (ECHR, 28 November 2011) 56.

105 European Court of Human Rights, *Guide on Article 2 of Protocol No. 1 to the European Convention on Human Rights* (30 April 2018) para (6)(c); *Sorabjee v. the United Kingdom* no 23938/94 (ECHR, 23 October 1995), *Jaramillo v. the United Kingdom* no 24865/94 (ECHR, 23 October 1995), *Dabhi v. the United Kingdom* no 28627/95 (ECHR, 17 January 1997).

106 *Ponomaryovi v. Bulgaria* App no 5335/05 (ECHR, 28 November 2011) 9.

107 *Ponomaryovi v. Bulgaria* App no 5335/05 (ECHR, 28 November 2011) 63.

108 *Ponomaryovi v. Bulgaria* App no 5335/05 (ECHR, 28 November 2011) 61.

109 Coram, Children's Legal Centre, *Immigration Bail and Studying Coram Children's Legal Centre's briefing* (March 2018) 5.

110 Much of the previous two subheadings are paraphrased, or taken from an article I had published in the International Journal for Research in Law: Ian Thomas Werrett, 'Does the United Kingdom's Immigration Act 2016 Deny People the Right to Education?' (2018) 3(4) International Journal for Research in Law 415

111 Reporters Without Borders, '2020 World Press Freedom Index' (*Reporters Without Borders*, 2020) <*https://rsf.org/en/ranking*> accessed 28/01/2021.

112 Home Office, *Hate Crime, England and Wales, 2019/20* (13 October 2020)

113 Home Office, *Hate Crime, England and Wales, 2019/20* (13 October 2020) 1.

114 College of Policing, *Hate Crime Operational Guidance* (May 2014) 32.

115 Home Office, *Hate Crime, England and Wales, 2019/20* (13 October 2020) 7.

116 See Chapter 1.

117 Ian Werrett, 'Protecting Vulnerable Children in Thailand' (2014) 17(1) Thailand Journal of Law and Policy <*http://thailawforum.com/articles/rights-of-refugee-children-in-thailand.html*> accessed 28/02/2021.

118 ECPAT, 'Child Trafficking in the UK 2020: A snapshot' <https://www.ecpat.org.uk/child-trafficking-in-the-uk-2020-snapshot#:~:text=ECPAT%20UK's%20new%20snapshot%20report, developments%20on%20this%20important%20issue> (*ECPAT*, October 2020) 7.

119 Dr Scott Blinder and Dr Lindsay Richards, 'UK Public Opinion toward Immigration: Overall Attitudes and Level of Concern' (*The Migration Observatory at the University of Oxford*, 20 January 2020) <*https://migrationobservatory.ox.ac.uk/resources/briefings/uk-public-opinion-toward-immigration-overall-attitudes-and-level-of-concern/*> accessed 28/01/2021.

120 Richard Keen and Vyara Apostolova, *Statistics on migrants and benefits* (House of Commons Paper No CBP 7445, 28 March 2017) <*https://commonslibrary.parliament.uk/research-briefings/cbp-7445/*> accessed 28/01/2021.

121 Christian Dustmann and Tommaso Frattini, 'The Fiscal Effects of Immigration to the UK' [2014] The Economic Journal (1) <https://www.cream-migration.org/files/FiscalEJ.pdf> 37.

122 Chris Belfield and Luke Sibieta, 'FE and sixth forms to suffer from 30 years without additional funding' (*Institute for Fiscal Studies*, 27 February 2017) < *https://www.ifs.org.uk/publications/8940*> accessed 28/02/21.

123 University and College Union, *Workload is an education issue* (2016) Key Findings, 5.

124 Department for Education, *Teacher Workload Survey 2019* (October 2019) 28.

125 Gov.UK, 'Maximum weekly working hours' <*https://www.gov.uk/maximum-weekly-working-hours*> accessed 28/01/2021.

126 University and College Union, *Workload is an education issue* (2016) Key Findings, 5.

127 Department for Education, *Teacher Workload Survey 2019* (October 2019) 29, 35.

128 University and College Union, *Workload is an education issue* (2016) 11.

129 Sofia Quaglia, 'Experts reveal the ideal number of hours you should work each week' (*Inverse*, 2 November 2020) <*https://www.inverse.com/mind-body/experts-reveal-the-ideal-number-of-hours-you-should-work-each-week*> accessed 28/01/2021; Andrew Merle, 'This is how many hours you should really be working' (*Altassian*, 1 December 2020) <*https://www.atlass ian.com/blog/productivity/this-is-how-many-hours-you-should-really-be-working*> accessed 28/02/2021.

130 Department for Education, *Teacher Workload Survey 2019* (October 2019) 28, 29, 35.

131 University and College Union, *Workload is an education issue* (2016) 4, 11.

132 University and College Union, *Workload is an education issue* (2016) 11.

133 University and College Union, *Workload is an education issue* (2016) 7, 33.

134 Department for Education, *Teacher Workload Survey 2019* (October 2019) 32.

135 Education International, 'UK: Retention crisis looming as teachers dissatisfied with pay conditions' (*Education International*, 26 February 2020) < *https://www.ei-ie.org/en/detail/16637/uk-retention-crisis-looming-as-tea chers-dissatisfied-with-pay-conditions?utm_source=dlvr.it&utm_medium=t witter*> accessed 28/01/2021.

136 Remi Adekoya, Eric Kaufmann and Thomas Simpson, 'Academic Freedom in the UK' (*Policy Exchange*, 2020) <*https://policyexchange.org.uk/publication/ academic-freedom-in-the-uk-2/*> 9, 12, 63.

137 Gov.uk, 'Universities to comply with free speech duties or face sanctions' (*Gov.UK*, 12 May 2021) <*https://www.gov.uk/government/news/univ*

ersities-to-comply-with-free-speech-duties-or-face-sanctions> accessed 12/05/2021

STATELESSNESS, TRAFFICKING AND HOW WE CAN HELP

138 Department of State, United States of America, *Trafficking in Persons Report 2020* (June 2020) 20.

139 Tanya Herring, 'Prevention and Protection Interventions for Stateless Non-Refugee and Forced Displaced Children' (2019) 31(2) New England Journal of Public Policy 5.

140 Some of details given here have been omitted to protect those still fleeing Burma.

141 Department of State, United States of America, *Trafficking in Persons Report 2020* (June 2020) 20.

142 Department of State, United States of America, *Trafficking in Persons Report 2020* (June 2020) 28.

143 Department of State, United States of America, *Trafficking in Persons Report 2020* (June 2020) 43.

144 Department of State, United States of America, *Trafficking in Persons Report 2020* (June 2020) 512.

145 Department of State, United States of America, *Trafficking in Persons Report 2020* (June 2020) 514.

146 Department of State, United States of America, *Trafficking in Persons Report 2020* (June 2020) 201.

147 Department of State, United States of America, *Trafficking in Persons Report 2020* (June 2020) 201.

148 United Nations Human Rights Office of the High Commissioner, 'Human Rights Dimension of Poverty' (*United Nations Human Rights Office of the High Commissioner*) <*https://www.ohchr.org/en/issues/poverty/dimensiono fpoverty/pages/index.aspx#:~:text=Poverty%20erodes%20or%20nullifies%20 economic,and%20the%20right%20to%20education.&text=It%20gives%20du e%20attention%20to,human%20dignity%20that%20accompany%20poverty .*> accessed 25/02/2021.

149 UNHCR UK, 'Europe' (*UNHCR*) <*https://www.unhcr.org/uk/europe-emergen cy.html*> accessed 25/02/2021.

150 Convention on the Rights of the Child 1989, art 7(1).

151 United Nations Treaty Collection, '11. Convention on the Rights of the Child' (*United Nations Treaty Collection*) <*https://treaties.un.org/Pages/View Details.aspx?src=TREATY&mtdsg_no=IV-11&chapter=4&clang=_en*> accessed 25/02/2021.

152 UNHCR 'Text of the 1961 Convention on the Reduction of Statelessness with an Introductory Note by the Office of the United Nations High Commissioner for Refugees' (May 2014) <*https://www.unhcr.org/ibelong/wp-content/uplo ads/1961-Convention-on-the-reduction-of-Statelessness_ENG.pdf*> 3.

153 The Protocol to Prevent, Suppress and Punish Trafficking in Persons Especially Women and Children, supplementing the United Nations Convention against Transnational Organized Crime 2000 3.

154 Ian Werrett, 'Protecting Vulnerable Children in Thailand' (2014) 17(1) Thailand Journal of Law and Policy <*http://thailawforum.com/articles/rights-of-refugee-children-in-thailand.html*> accessed 28/02/2021.

CHALLENGING DISCRIMINATION, CONFLICT AND POVERTY.

155 Burmese Rohingya Organisation UK, *The Right to Education Denied for Rohingya Refugees in Bangladesh* (December 2018) 3.

156 Burmese Rohingya Organisation UK, 'The Right to Education Denied for Rohingya Refugees in Bangladesh (*burmacampaign.org.uk*, December 2018) <https://burmacampaign.org.uk/media/The-Right-to-Education-Denied-for-Rohingya-Refugees-in-Bangladesh.pdf> 4–5.

157 Burmese Rohingya Organisation UK, 'The Right to Education Denied for Rohingya Refugees in Bangladesh (*burmacampaign.org.uk*, December 2018) <https://burmacampaign.org.uk/media/The-Right-to-Education-Denied-for-Rohingya-Refugees-in-Bangladesh.pdf> 7–8.

158 General Assembly, 'Situation of Human Rights in Myanmar' (Seventy-second Session, on 8 September 2017) UN Doc A/72/382, paras 47–48, 83(a).

159 General Assembly, 'Resolution Adopted by the General Assembly on 27 December 2019' 'Situation of human rights of Rohingya Muslims and other minorities in Myanmar' (15 January 2020) UN Doc A/RES/74/246 4.

160 Security Council Report, 'Chronology of Events: Myanmar' (*Security Council Report.org*) <*https://www.securitycouncilreport.org/chronology/myanmar.ph p*> accessed 13/03/2021.

161 UNHCR UK, 'Educate A Child' (*UNHCR UK*) <*https://www.unhcr.org/uk/educ ate-a-child.html*> accessed 13/03/2021.

162 UNHCR, *Raising the Bar: Promising Practices for Refugee Education from UNHCR and Educate A Child* (September 2020) Syria, Pakistan.

163 Laura Vega and Monisha Bajaj, 'The right to education in protracted conflict: teachers' experiences in non-formal education in Colombia' (2016) 14(3) Globalisation, Societies and Education 358–373, 360–361.

164 Enrique Patiño, 'Opportunities on the move are opportunities to learn' (*UNICEF Latin America and the Caribbean*, 16 August 2019) <*https://www.unic ef.org/lac/en/stories/opportunities-move-are-opportunities-learn*> accessed 13/03/2021.

165 Malala Fund, 'Education Champion Network' (*Malala.org*) <*https://malala.o rg/champions?sc=header*> accessed 13/03/2021.

166 Malala Fund, 'Advocacy' (*Malala.org*) <https://malala.org/advocacy> accessed 13/03/2021.

167 United Nations, '4 ensure inclusive and equitable quality education and promote lifelong learning opportunities for all' (*United Nations Department of Economic and Social Affairs*) <*https://sdgs.un.org/goals/goal4*> accessed 14/03/2021.

168 The World Bank, *World Development Report 2018 – Learning to Realize Education's Promise* (2018) 58.

169 The World Bank, 'Education' (*The World Bank*) <*https://www.worldbank.org/ en/topic/education/overview*> accessed 14/03/2021.

170 The World Bank, *World Development Report 2018 – Learning to Realize Education's Promise* (2018) 60–62.

171 The World Bank, *World Development Report 2018 – Learning to Realize Education's Promise* (2018) 189.

172 UNESCO, *Education 2030: Incheon Declaration and Framework for Action* (2015) 9.

173 General Assembly, 'Second United Nations Development Decade' (Twenty-fifth session, 16 October 1970) UN Doc A/8124 and Add.1 para 43.

174 Malala Fund, *Financing at Full Force* (June 2019) 12.

175 UNESCO, *Education 2030: Incheon Declaration and Framework for Action* (2015) 37.

176 The World Bank, 'Government expenditure on education total (% of government expenditure)' (*The World Bank*) <*https://data.worldbank.org/indicator/ SE.XPD.TOTL.GB.ZS*> accessed 14/03/2021.

177 OECD, 'Data: Net ODA' (*OECD*) <*https://data.oecd.org/oda/net-oda.htm#indicator-chart*> accessed on 10/11/2020.

178 UNESCO, *Policy Paper 31: Aid to education is stagnating and not going to countries most in need* (May 2017) 1–3.

MAKING 1948'S DREAM A REALITY

179 Convention on the Rights of the Child 1989, art 28(3).

180 United Nations, *Policy Brief: Education during COVID-19 and beyond* (August 2020) 2–13.

181 Cathy Li and Farah Lalani, 'The COVID-19 pandemic has changed education forever. This is how' (*World Economic Forum*, 29 April 2020) <https://www.weforum.org/agenda/2020/04/coronavirus-education-global-covid19-online-digital-learning/> accessed 20/03/2021.

182 United Nations, *Policy Brief: Education during COVID-19 and beyond* (August 2020) 14.

183 United Nations, *Policy Brief: Education during COVID-19 and beyond* (August 2020) 14–15.

184 United Nations, *Policy Brief: Education during COVID-19 and beyond* (August 2020) 4, 24.

185 Ben Taylor, 'study abroad for free? 11 European Countries where Masters tuition is free (or almost free) in 2020/21' (*findamasters*, 31 January 2020) <*https://www.findamasters.com/advice/blog/1598/study-abroad-for-free-11-european-countries-where-masters-tuition-is-free-or-almost-free-in-2020-21*> accessed 11/11/20.

186 IPSA, 'MP's Pay and Pensions' (*IPSA*) <*https://www.theipsa.org.uk/mp-costs/mps-pay-and-pensions/*> accessed 18/11/2020.

187 Education Support, *Teacher Wellbeing Index 2019* (*Education Support*, 2019) <*https://www.educationsupport.org.uk/resources/research-reports/teacher-wellbeing-index-2019*> accessed 25/11/2020.

188 Universal Declaration of Human Rights 1948, art 26(2).

189 Convention on the Rights of the Child 1989, art 29(1)(B).

190 History.co.uk, *The Caribbean, Indian and African RAF pilots of WW2* (History.co.uk) <*https://www.history.co.uk/article/the-rafs-caribbean-%2520Indian-and-African-pilots-of-ww2*> accessed 13/05/2021

191 Mariusz Gasior, *The Polish pilots who flew in the Battle of Britain* (iwn.org) <*https://www.iwm.org.uk/history/the-polish-pilots-who-flew-in-the-battle-*

of-britain> accessed 13/05/2021

Printed in Great Britain
by Amazon